THE
BRAIDED RUG
BOOK

Country Kitchen

I believe in cord wood, iron stoves, and breakfast
I believe in freshly baked bread and mail order catalogues,
ticking clocks, dogs and cats and corn right out of the garden.
I believe in families who laugh together and because of this
I believe in tomorrow and the day after and the goodness of man
       and the joy of living.
                —Maxwell Mays

THE
BRAIDED RUG
BOOK

CREATING YOUR OWN
AMERICAN FOLK ART

Revised Edition

NORMA M. STURGES
ELIZABETH J. STURGES

LARK BOOKS
A Division of Sterling Publishing Co., Inc.
New York

Editors:
Deborah Morgenthal, Susan Kieffer

Art Directors:
Kathy Holmes, Kay Holmes Stafford

Cover Designer:
Barbara Zaretsky

Associate Art Director:
Shannon Yokeley

Art Production Assistant:
Jeff Hamilton

Editorial Assistance:
Delores Gosnell, Dawn Dillingham

Illustrators:
Caroline Cleaveland, Orrin Lundgren

Photographer:
Michael Drejza
Front cover photograph © Glen Janssen

Cover Credits:

Front Cover
Norma Sturges, *The Marly Rose*

Back Cover, Top Left
Braiding clamp

Top Right
Janice Jurta, *Multi-Corde Bound Braided Rug*

Bottom Right
Lucy Long Armour, *Cirque*

Bottom Left
Janice Jurta, *Multi-Corde Rectangular Braided Rug*

Sturges, Norma M.
    The braided rug book : creating your own American folk art / Norma M. Sturges, Elizabeth J. Sturges. — Rev. ed.
        p. cm.
    Includes bibliographical references and index.
    ISBN 1-57990-880-2 (pbk.)
    1. Rugs, Braided. I. Sturges, Elizabeth J., 1952- II. Title.
TT850.S87 2006
746.7'3—dc22   2006009151

10 9 8 7 6 5 4 3 2 1

Revised Edition

Published by Lark Books, A Division of
Sterling Publishing Co., Inc.
387 Park Avenue South, New York, N.Y. 10016

Text © 2006, Norma M. Sturges and Elizabeth J. Sturges
Photography © 2006, Lark Books, except as noted
Illustrations © 2006, Lark Books, except as noted

Distributed in Canada by Sterling Publishing,
c/o Canadian Manda Group, 165 Dufferin Street
Toronto, Ontario, Canada M6K 3H6

Distributed in the United Kingdom by GMC Distribution Services,
Castle Place, 166 High Street, Lewes, East Sussex, England BN7 1XU

Distributed in Australia by Capricorn Link (Australia) Pty Ltd.,
P.O. Box 704, Windsor, NSW 2756 Australia

If you have questions or comments about this book, please contact:
Lark Books
67 Broadway
Asheville, NC 28801
(828) 253-0467

Manufactured in China

ISBN 13: 978-1-57990-880-5
ISBN 10: 1-57990-880-2

For information about custom editions, special sales, premium and corporate purchases, please contact Sterling Special Sales Department at 800-805-5489 or specialsales@sterlingpub.com.

CONTENTS

Dedicated to

▼ ▼ ▼

The talented women of the
Rocky Mountain Rug Braiders' Guild,
whose lives and stories
have been laced together with our rugs.

Braiding retreat, Salida, Colorado, 2005

Author Biography

▼ ▼ ▼

Norma Sturges has been braiding and designing rugs for over 50 years, developing and refining her style along the way. For many years she taught braiding at Arrapahoe Community College in Littleton, Colorado, in the adult education program, and at Quilts in the Attic. She has demonstrated her craft and exhibited her rugs at country fairs and crafts exhibitions too numerous to count. She was one of the early entrants in the *Directory of American Craftsmen*, published in 1988 by *Early American Life* magazine, and her work has appeared in *Country Home* magazine, *Rug Hooking* magazine, and the *Denver Post*. She has three children, seven grandchildren, and one great-grandchild. She lives in Littleton, Colorado, with her husband Ed.

Elizabeth Sturges lives in Denver with her daughter. She has her MBA from the University of Colorado and is an elementary school lead teacher in the Denver public schools. Norma credits her daughter and co-author for recognizing the need to teach classes in order to keep the special art of braiding alive. She has been the promoter, encourager, and helper with all of the shows, and collaborator on both books.

Acknowledgments

▼ ▼ ▼

I would like to give credit to my husband Ed Sturges for 60 years of support, and whose idea it was to write the original *Braided Rug Book*. Our homes, from Connecticut to Colorado, have always had a braided rug on the hearth and in every room as well.

This revised edition brings many old and new supportive friends to thank and to acknowledge. For contributing to the success of the first book, I again thank Jane and George Sturges for their assistance, friendship, and encouragement. Thanks also to Tangy Buchanan, who arranged my rugs in the family-owned Stewart-Buchanan Antiques and who recommended photographer Mike Drejza. And thanks to Susan Stewart, who did the first edition's typing and who was a sounding board as I went along, and Caroline Cleaveland, a former student, who did the illustrations.

Many thanks to the staff at Lark Books: Susan Mowery Kieffer, my editor, for her patience and understanding; Deborah Morgenthal, the editor of the original *Braided Rug Book* and now editor in chief and vice president, and Carol Taylor, president and publisher. Lark's support of the braided rug has been critical in the revival of the craft.

Craft people build on one another's ideas, and so my thanks to the braiders who have forwarded the craft through published works. My appreciation to my students and other braiders for their encouragement. I am deeply grateful to the many talented braiders whose rugs are included in my books and whose works serve to inspire.

The Rocky Mountain Rug Braiders' Guild has been a tremendous source of support and inspiration. Special thanks to founders Helen Nielsen, Janet Fox, Janice Watson, and Robbie Mallin for their early vision. I appreciate the enthusiastic support of Beverly Sullivan, Lois Elliot, June Kittelson, Doris Cruze, Karen Kafka, Betty Everett, Rise Hames, Karol Marquez, and the other members who have shared their hearts, homes, and friendship. With our various talents, the Rocky Mountain Rug Braiders' Guild is spreading the joy of braiding.

Special mention needs to be given to the following five national braiding experts:

Nancy Young, a long-time leader in the revival of this craft, who has generously shared her Maine home, vision, and expertise with hundreds of students through her camps, newsletters, and teaching.

Anne Eastwood, an artistic, nationally acclaimed, Florida rug hooking and braiding teacher whose presence every summer at the Salida Rug Braiding Retreat is greatly appreciated.

Maxine Ward, a gracious southern braider from Arkansas, who has forwarded the craft with her multi-strand rugs.

Verna Cox who has influenced generations of braiders with her publications and videos. I used her 1967, *Manual on Braided Rugs*, for many years in my classes.

Marie Griswold, whose husband, Rodger, invented Braid-Aids in 1947. Their braided rug business was the source for braiding supplies for more than 50 years.

Also, I am most grateful to:

Dori Kupko my oldest daughter who, as a baby, inspired my very first braided rug for her nursery and for whom a braided rug still remains an important symbol of our homes and family.

Amy Kupko Underwood, who delighted us with the gift of great-granddaughter Marly Rose-a fourth generation of our family to inspire the creation of, and grow up with the warmth of, homemade braided rugs.

Megan Kupko, whose request for a wedding gift was, first our presence at her wedding and second, anything that was handmade or meaningful to us, the guests. Of course, I gave her a special braided rug.

Granddaughter Rebecca Sturges Murray, now a talented Parsons School of Design student, who was the inspiration for the *Peter Rabbit Nursery Rug*. We adore her enthusiasm and support. She is our "in house" consultant for all things design.

And finally, many, many thanks to my daughter Elizabeth (Betsy) Sturges for her constant love, encouragement, enthusiasm, and invaluable help. The rugs and experiences in this book are mine, but these words are hers.

✺ SUBJECT OF THE BOOK ✺

Since 1830, American families have treasured their braided rugs. They are a symbol of hearth, home, comfort, family, and love. The braided rug is a unique American craft.

Prior to the publication of my first book, everywhere I went someone would share a special loving memory of her grandmother's rugs. Grandmothers may have handed down their rugs but not their knowledge and art of the craft. I was determined to be the grandmother who was going to change that.

The past 10 years have brought together braiders throughout the United States who have reinvigorated this art form by teaching, sharing, and pushing the creative boundaries of braided rugs. In this book, you will see photos of inspiring rugs created by some of the country's best braiders.

The book includes a brief history, illustrated with historic photographs, and it offers new instructions and color designs for braiding your own beautiful rugs.

Grandmothers, as you know, are persistent women. People of all ages are enjoying the revival of this wonderful craft. I am a great-grandmother, determined to see that we braid the stories of our generations together into rugs that we continue to treasure.

Sturges Family Christmas card, 1954

Introduction

▼ ▼ ▼

Braiding rugs is an American tradition that, as with many crafts, developed out of a need and developed into an art.

It was kept alive in the 20th century to enrich homes with a timeless quality, compatible with decor of many styles.

A braided rug is a satisfying, personal, artistic expression, and may well turn out to become an heirloom, passed on from generation to generation. Above all, a braided rug is an object of beauty, with the unmistakable warmth, richness of texture, and depth of color that only pure wool, braided with care, can deliver.

Technically, a braided rug is three *strands* of wool, with their edges turned in, joined by repeatedly pulling the right *tube* to center position and then the left—just the way you braid hair. The *continuous braid* is then *laced*, or sewn, together.

In the early days of braiding, old clothing was used to make rugs. Today, any type of fabric or fiber can be used, but the strength of wool makes it the best choice for a long-wearing rug.

Wool coats with torn pockets or faded colors can be rejuvenated; colors come back to life after seams are opened and the coat is washed in the washing machine. Recycled in this way, the old wool faces a longer life than if it had remained a coat.

However, today's rug braiders usually don't have the time to take apart clothing. Fortunately, there are sources available for purchasing new, reasonably priced wool. The equipment needed is minimal: a clamp, lacing thread and needle, and probably Braid-Aids (used to fold in the edges of the wool strands).

I have been braiding for more than 50 years, developing and refining my own style and technique along the way. Each of my rugs has been inspired by a unique need or vision, and, as such, is an integral part of my family's history and of my own development as a crafts person. I'm very possessive of my rugs. Each is interwoven with fond memories. Braiding also has served as an outlet for creative expression, providing me with a great deal of satisfaction.

My first attempt at braiding occurred while I was awaiting the birth of my first child, Dorie. I envisioned a cozy, old-fashioned nursery with a pink and blue braided rug.

Although I loved this rug for sentimental reasons, it really didn't turn out that well. I had no pattern, no teacher, and could find little information on how to turn my dream into reality. The following year, I attended the Eastern States Exposition, the fair for all of the New England States, where the best of all aspects of New England country living are displayed. I was able to obtain a pattern and begin braiding in earnest.

Now I am the one teaching classes in rug braiding and demonstrating braiding at country fairs and crafts exhibitions. Although teaching is very rewarding, I wanted to find a way to encourage more would-be braiders. I'm certain that somewhere across the country there are many, many people eager as I was to make a braided rug but who lack the necessary information.

This book represents my desire to share braiding with a wide audience. The rugs and patterns you'll find here will allow you to create beautiful rugs for your home and family. All of the patterns come with complete instructions and can be executed in your choice of colors. Other rugs are presented in different sizes with individual color plans. For the adventurous, there are even hexagon, strip, three-circle, scalloped, watermelon, and multi-strand rugs.

When you braid a rug by hand for a special place or person, you take part in the long tradition of making functional, one-of-a-kind works of art. The welcome rug (braided, of course) has been rolled out for you. I invite you to enter the world of braiding and find out how simple and satisfying this time-honored craft can be.

History

▼   ▼   ▼

*T*he braided rug is truly an American discovery— a *folk art*, made by "folks" nearly 170 years ago.

According to authors Jean Lipman and Alice Winchester (*The Flowering of American Folk Art 1776–1876*),

"Folk Art had some common denominators - independence from cosmopolitan, academic traditions; lack of formal training, which made for interest in design…a simple and unpretentious rather than sophisticated approach, originating more typically in rural rather than urban places and from craft rather than fine-art traditions."

Anyone who has family or friends who braid may recognize those characteristics in their rugs and in their creators.

Braiders today have the qualities consistent with Lipman and Winchester's definition of a folk artist of the previous century, that is, someone with "a sense of personal commitment to the work and of pleasure, even excitement, in carrying it out in a fresh, free way."

The Emergence of Braided Rugs as Floor Coverings

In the 1700s, early American homes had wooden floors covered with straw, corn husks, and rush woven mats. In 1750, the first carpets appeared, but only the very wealthy could afford these imports. Loom-woven rag carpets were made in the late 1700s. By 1816, painted floor cloths were very popular.

Although braided rugs are often associated with the colonial era, the craft did not develop until the early 19th century. Like three strands of wool braided together, there are three factors that account for the development of rug braiding: the popularity of braided straw bonnets and floor mats, an interest among homemakers in floor covering, and the introduction of local factories producing woolen fabric.

In the late 1700s, straw bonnets and floor mats were braided in Providence, Rhode Island, and in the neighboring Massachusetts towns. This craft then spread to Maine. Many women in these communities earned money braiding straw bonnets. By the early 1800s in New England, there were 24 "manufactories" producing woolen fabric, many of them in the same towns where straw braiding was done. Wool was now readily accessible in America and was favored for floor coverings because it was more durable than cotton or straw and more beautiful as well. The development of the power loom in 1839 made available commercially produced car-

"Straw Hat Maker," *Little Book of Early American Crafts & Trades*

pets. Manufactured rugs were too expensive to be purchased by the general public, but they did have the effect of heightening interest in attractive floor coverings. Thrifty, but clever, New England housewives, who already knew how to braid, were inspired to create a new craft for their homes: the braided rug.

The earliest braided rugs date from the 1820s in New England. During this time, homemakers started experimenting with many types of rug, including braided, hooked, embroidered, needlepoint, yarn sewn, and shirred. According to Sally Clarke Carty (*How to Make Braided Rugs*), the first recorded braided rug was made by a Miss M. Locke of Andover, Massachusetts. She won two dollars at the Essex Agriculture Show in 1827 for her rug that the judges described as a "very pretty braided rag rug."

The craft continued to proliferate throughout the 19th century; as Americans traveled across the prairies in covered wagons during the westward expansion, they transported a few treasured possessions—including their braided rugs. In fact, these rugs became the pioneers' primary floor coverings.

In the early 20th century, the braided rug enjoyed an upsurge of interest; widely promoted by interior designers and the new, upscale home magazines, braided rugs were praised as purely decorative items, rather than as an inexpensive way to cover floors. Showcasing intricate shapes and the color pallet of the day, braided rugs achieved a design height never again equalled.

From the 1960s through the 1970s, the braided rug lost some prestige and fell outside the mainstream of design; as a result, expert rug braiders became a rarity. Fortunately, today braided rugs are rapidly resuming their original function as items with a dual attraction: they are beautiful and they fulfill a real need.

Perhaps their greatest appeal for us today lies in their symbolism, in that they evoke images of a simpler era when home, family, and friends were unchallenged as the central elements of our lives.

The Wallace Nutting Connection

Wallace Nutting was an American minister who retired in 1904 at the age of 44 and turned his prodigious talents to taking photographs, collecting antique furniture, making reproduction furniture, restoring vintage homes, and writing.

It is for his photography and writing that we braiders are grateful; his photographs of the interiors of colonial homes, published in his States series books titled *Beautiful Connecticut*, *Beautiful Massachusetts* (and New York, New Hampshire, Maine, Vermont, Pennsylvania, and Florida) captured for posterity the enduring beauty of braided rugs.

During his photographic period, it is said that he took 50,000 scenes in New England, Europe, and the Near East. He reproduced 1,000 different photographs millions of times. By 1936, ten million Nutting photographs had been sold. Most of his New England photographs were of apple blossoms, streams, stone walls, country lanes, and homes. Fortunately, he also took many interior photos, arranged by his wife, of great New England colonials, showing the furniture and decor of the early 1900s. A wide variety of braided rugs are showcased; there are medium-sized scattered braided rugs, very large, room-sized braided rugs, and many interesting shapes that are rarely seen today. For instance, a photograph he took in the Webb house in Withersfield, Connecticut shows a very large, sophisticated rug with nine circles combined to make one rug.

He generally decorated the rooms with ovals and circles of various sizes. These shapes, then and now, are by far the most popular. His photograph called "The Quilting Party" has a three-circle braided rug on the floor. This rug inspired me to make my own three-circle rug, called "Heather Roses" (page 89).

Several of his photographs show women, dressed in colonial clothing, braiding rugs. The technique for the rug shown in the Rug Maker on page 12 was to keep braiding

1930s ten-strand braided rug with swirl effect

Above: Wallace Nutting,
The Rug Maker

Left: Wallace Nutting,
The Quilting Party

until you had a large pile of braid and then sew the braid into a rug. We call this a *hit-or-miss* type rug. It was as popular then as it is today.

Nutting articulated his philosophy on floor coverings in *Connecticut Beautiful*: "One may mix the braided and the hooked rugs, or the hooked and Turkish rugs, but braided rugs form too strong a contrast with Oriental rugs. Large rugs are more desirable by far. The effect of many patches is bad."

In 1904, he and his wife, Mariet Griswold, bought a beautiful farm in Southbury, Connecticut, and named it Nuttinghame. This farm was his headquarters for eight years. Photographs of his home reveal a collection of braided rugs. One of his most famous interiors, shown below, was his own living room at Nuttinghame. He photographed it so many times and sold so many of these images that he said his living room paid for the farm.

His appreciation of braided rugs aside, my interest in Nutting is personal, as well. My mother-in-law, then Eula Curtiss, was photographed by him in 1909 wearing colonial period dress . Her picture, "Who's In the Parlor" (right), is one of the first interior photographs in his *Connecticut Beautiful* book. He photographed her in Woodbury, Connecticut, in a home owned by her grandfather, Daniel Curtiss, who bought the house in 1834. The mirror she is looking into is also one of my family's treasured possessions.

Fred Thompson of Portland, Maine, and David Davidson of Providence, Rhode Island, also photographed in the same period and region, using the same technique—black and white photographs, hand-painted by women colorists. Braided rugs feature prominently in their photographs, too. We are fortunate to have this pictorial record to document the appeal braided rugs had for early Americans.

Above right: Wallace Nutting, *Who's in the Parlor?*

Right: Wallace Nutting, *Proposing an Amendment to the Linen*

Braided Rugs as a Shaker Craft

The Shakers, whose formal name is the United Society of Believers in Christ's Second Appearing, are a religious sect founded by Ann Lee, an English factory worker. She and her eight followers came to America in 1774. After years of persecution and hardship, the sect, at its peak in the 1840s, grew to about 6,000 members in 18 separate communities. The Shakers believed they could experience God and His love directly, and that in their striving for perfection, they could live as if the kingdom of heaven were already manifest on earth. They practiced equality of the sexes, separation from the world, hierarchy of authority, and celibacy. Hard work was also a tenet of the Shaker religion. Author Beverly Gordon (*Shaker Textile Arts*) quotes Mother Ann, as Ann Lee was called, telling her followers to "put your hands to work and your hearts to God."

This philosophy and their cloistered lifestyle produced communities distinguished by fine craftsmanship in their buildings, furniture, baskets, and textiles. They also invented much of the equipment used in their everyday life. The Shakers were encouraged to keep journals to record their time and ideas. Their sales and purchase records were also preserved so that we know that in 1838, in Watervliet, New York, they made 40 dozen braided sashes for sale.

Starting in 1840, the Shakers made impressive rugs of many types: braided, crocheted, hooked, shirred, and knitted. It was in their rugs that the Shakers could express their love of color and design; in their rugs, their creativity could blossom.

The Shakers made brightly colored braided rugs with small, tight braids. Their braids were plaited (a flat braid with the fold on the back), and they laced the rows together by lacing every other loop. They made the usual three-strand braid but also did up to a seven-strand braid. They made interestingly shaped rugs, such as the eight-scalloped rug below.

The Shakers also had a strong sensitivity to color and blended colors subtly, alternating dark and light rows in concentric rings. They loved borders and used borders within borders. In fact, braided borders became a recognizable Shaker trademark. This design element was practical as well as beautiful, because braid is strong and protects the edges of a rug.

The Shaker Museum in Chatham, New York houses three outstanding examples of Shaker rug making: circular, made from brightly colored dyed yarn, they are flat-knitted in bands that are butted or joined together. Their elaborate patterns and design give an Aztec or Indian appearance. These rugs are also bordered by up to three to four rows of braid—either a three- or five-strand braid. Another of these knitted circular rugs is in the collection of Robert Booth; on the back of the rug is written, "Made 1892 by Sister Elvira in her 88th year." These rugs are truly remarkable works of art that haven't been surpassed to this day.

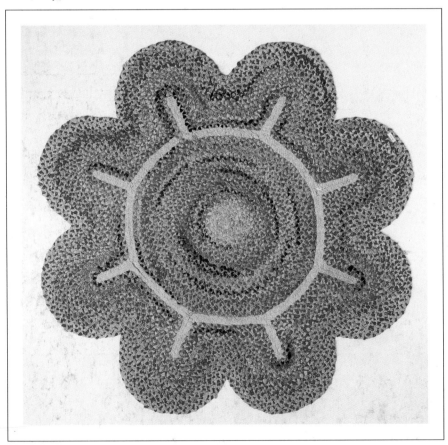

Shaker scalloped braided rug, Hancock Shaker Village Collection, Pittsfield, Massachusetts. Photographer: Paul Rocheleau

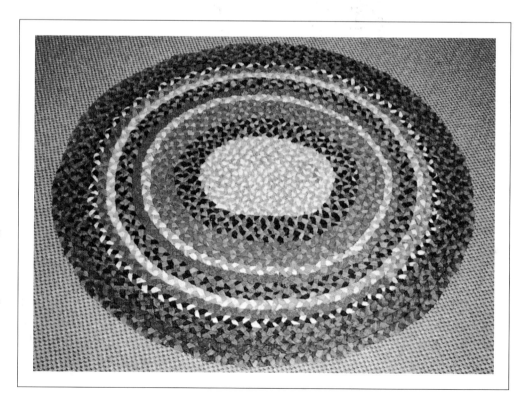

Above: Shaker knitted rug with braided border, Shaker Museum, Chatham, New York

Right: Shaker braided rug, Shaker Museum, Chatham, New York

A Braided Rug Scrapbook

▼ ▼ ▼

My family moved to Woodbury, Connecticut, a beautifully preserved colonial town, when I was in my early teens. It was a peaceful village of picturesque homes filled with antiques, braided rugs, and other examples of family crafts.

"Antiques are what link this generation to those before," I have heard. I believe this is also true of crafts such as rug braiding.

Whenever I demonstrate, people always come up to me and wistfully say, "I remember my grandmother, mother, or father braiding." Often I can detect in people the desire to carry on the tradition of braiding. But they don't know how to take that first step.

All braiders have stories about the first rug they made, or about braided rugs they have saved, or about those that got away. Every braider has to make a first rug. It may not turn out to be a showpiece, but it is treasured because it represents a courageous plunge into something new.

Here are a few of my favorite stories about braiders and the special rugs they bravely created.

Old Sparhawk

When I first started braiding in 1949, I saw a rug I thought was the most beautiful I could imagine—9-x-12-feet (2.8 x 3.7 m) with wonderful colors. I talked to the people at the Old Sparhawk Mill in Portland, Maine where the rug was

made, and they sent me a pattern. One of my first students, Doris Newell, made it for her living room. Doris loved to braid but didn't like to lace the braid together. So she would braid and braid, and I would go over, almost on a daily basis, sit on the floor, and lace a round or so. (I don't lace on the floor anymore!)

I made a smaller version for Ed, my then six-year-old son, to use in his knotty pine bedroom. This was one rug that did wear out; he also wore out his wooden bureau, so I didn't feel too badly.

A few years ago, I got the urge to make a version of this same rug. It combines old red, maroon, light and medium green, medium blue, blue-gray, brown, black, gold, and beige. I've named this rug "Old Sparhawk" in honor of the mill that inspired me many years ago.

16

Jane Sturges and Her Mother, Ruth Platt

In 1955, I started teaching a few friends in Woodbury, Connecticut to braid. In the winter of 1957, my sister-in-law, Jane Platt Sturges, wanted me to teach a class at the Southbury Training School where she was a social worker. There were 22 in the class including her mother, her aunt, her cousin, her best friend, and many other personnel from the training school. We met all winter in the cafeteria. It was a great place with plenty of tables and good lighting. Some of these individuals made room-sized rugs. Jane's was quite distinctive—a circle with a tiny firm braid. She started with shades of light blue and changed to dark blue in about seven rows, then switched to a light gold to dark orange/rust, then switched to greens and reds, following the same light to dark pattern. I photographed this rug after it had been on the floor for 35 years. Its colors are still perfect. However, with hard wear it flattened out—as flat as the hardwood floor it sits on. It is a beautiful one-of-a-kind rug, as are all individually designed rugs.

Jane's mother, Ruth Platt, was an amazing woman. When we met, she was a widow caring for 15 retarded adults who lived in the wing of her large farmhouse. She was a wonderful cook; I still remember her sticky buns! She braided one rug and became so infatuated with the craft that she started selling rug wool out of her barn. Later, she turned the farm over to a daughter, bought an old colonial house in Woodbury, Connecticut and built a shop on the back. From the time she was 60 until she was 70, she sold rug wool and other fabric out of her Fabric Barn, as the shop was called. At the age of 81, she finished another rug. She made this 6-foot (1.8 m) hit-or-miss rug for her son.

A Salesman's Sample

In 1957 I made a salesman's sample rug. In those days, the woolen mills wove many yards of fabric for tailors, using every color combination they could weave. If the tailor wanted a certain color combination, he would cut a piece out of the wool and attach it to his order. Braiders sometimes were able to use what was left of the bolt.

This combination of beautifully blended wool made great rugs. My rug had a mosaic look to it, and I gave it to my sister-in-law, Jane. She has enjoyed it for the past 37 years, and it is just starting to show wear.

Reclaiming Dori's Rug

When my oldest daughter Dori was about eight, I made her a 6-x-8-foot (1.8 x 2.5 m) braided rug in dusty rose, pink, gray, beige, and camel to match her bedspread and curtains. It remained her bedroom rug through college when we sold our Massachusetts home. I shipped the rug to her in Colorado for Amy, her five-year-old daughter. Amy's bedroom was small, but it worked well until baby sister Megan arrived to share her bedroom. Dori and her husband Buzz bought a larger house but didn't have a place for the rug. Dori agreed to let us borrow it. I brought it home and gave it a place of prominence on our bedroom floor. The taupe and dusty rose colors match our room perfectly, and I have enjoyed it on a daily basis ever since.

Ed and the Case of the Missing Rug

In 1978, we sold our great old New England colonial in Massachusetts and put our furniture in storage—except, of course, I took my braided rugs with me. We visited our son Ed in Connecticut for a few weeks and then came on to Denver. My husband Ed got a job in Vail, and our possessions were shipped there. When I unpacked, I realized the rug I was working on was missing. A few months later, my son moved to Vail, too; he drove out, followed closely by a truck carrying his furniture. We were waiting to help him unload when this large, open truck came into view with a 4-foot (1.2 m) braid flapping from the side. "Well, there's my rug," I said, with a mixture of relief and dismay. Dangling out was the gold, cream, and beige section of the rug. The 2,100-mile trip apparently didn't harm it. I cite this story when people wonder if braided rugs are fragile.

(Another common concern is how to clean them; this rug has never been cleaned and has been on the floor for 16 years.)

I call this rug "Aspen," as it is just the color of the gorgeous aspens we so enjoyed in Vail.

Our Christmas Card—1989

Every year I try to find Christmas cards with scenes that include braided rugs in the setting to send to friends. Sometimes I photograph my own. I call this my "Poinsettia" rug because the red is the exact shade of the red poinsettia. The rug uses my "Americana" pattern, substituting red and green for blue, gray, red, and plaid.

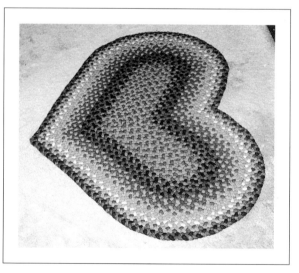

Home is Where the Heart is

When Ed married Jayne, I gave them the first heart rug I had made, and it has been by their bed or at the front door ever since. When I demonstrate, the heart seems to be the most admired rug.

A Peter Rabbit Rug for Bets

When my daughter Bets was planning her nursery, she and I bought pastel gingham and calico cotton to make a crib quilt. She wanted a Beatrix Potter theme, so I bought a Wedgewood lamp with Peter Rabbit in the briar patch and designed a rug from this lamp.

When her daughter Rebecca was little, she loved to creep on this rug, enjoying the texture and the many pastel colors. When she was about two-and-a-half years old, her mother explained to her that I had made the rug for her. When I came over, she said, "Grandma, you made this rug for me—thank you!" With delight, she realized that I had also made

the braided hit-or-miss rug in their front hall. Then she pointed to their oriental rug in the living room and asked, "And, Grandma, did you make this one, too?"

As it turned out, I had to make this nursery rug again; it became pretty awkward taking it off her nursery room floor every time I wanted to show it. It is 5-x-7 feet (1.5 x 2.2 m), and at an hour a day took me more than three months to make. The photographs of the rug's development show how the look changes with the addition of new colors.

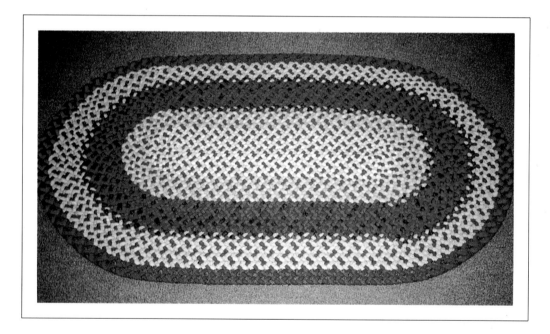

Men Do Braid

I haven't taught many men. Quite often they express an interest, but being the lone male in a class with ten women can be a challenge. One fellow met that challenge. Jim Armstrong does cable maintenance and installation repair for a telephone company. He loved braiding and would stop at thrift stores and tell me about the great blankets he found. Once he was sent to Wyoming for a special job. He packed his tool chest with wool and braided in the motel room in the evening. He got a bit of kidding from his buddies, but he held up. Jim has gone from this first rug to demonstrating the craft at local fairs and festivals.

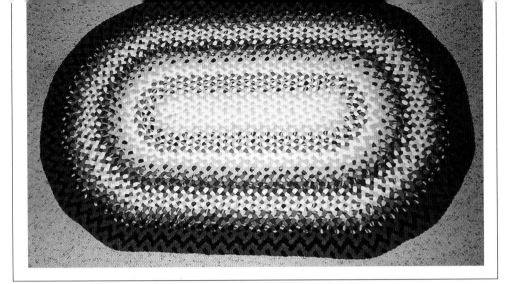

Winter Hues Fleece Rug

Janica Behnke likes to braid with fleece. She finds it very versatile, quicker to braid with than wool, easy to wash, and the fleece can be found in a great range of colors. Winter Hues measures 39 x 61 inches (99.1 x 154.9 cm).

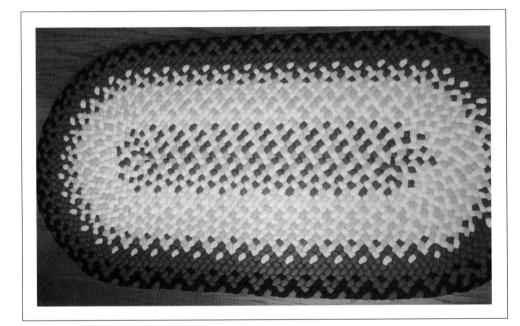

A Two-by-Four Arrow

Terri Donica runs a small business called The Heirloom Wool Room from her home in Mitchell, Indiana, where she makes and sells custom rugs and teaches classes as well. Her black and white oval rug is 24 x 48 inches (61 x 121.9 cm) and is laced with linen-flax twine.

Blueberry Hill Hexagon Rug

Trisha Altman is a long-time braider. She took classes with Barbara Fisher and has now taught hundreds of braiders herself. Tricia created this 29 x 59-inch (73.7 x 149.9 cm) three-hexagon rug with border.

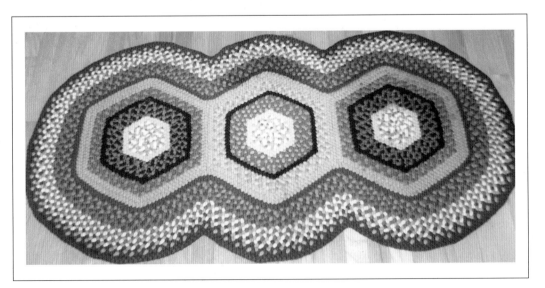

Sparkling in Plaid

Traudi Bestler teaches at North House Folk School in Minnesota. She likes to use plaids because she feels they add some "sparkle" to her rugs. This creation measures 39 x 54 inches (99.1 x 137.2 cm).

This Rug is My Rug

Lois Elliott collected 1930s reproduction prints for a quilt design and decided to make a braided rug to match. She named the rug "My Rug" because all the other rugs she has made over the years have been claimed by family members.

Patriotic Heart

Lynn Hafer is great with color combinations, and she makes beautiful, tight braids. Her heart-shaped rug measures 27 x 43 inches (68 x 109.2 cm).

Connie's Heart

Jocelyn Jaquiery has saved wool since she was a teenager. She found *The Braided Rug Book* in the library shortly after its publication. After paying overdue fines three times, she finally bought the book and has became a self-taught braider in New Zealand. The length of Jocelyn's rug pictured here is 49 inches (124.5 cm).

Jayne's Rug Story, by Karen Kafka

My daughter Jayne lives in a small apartment with a wood floor in the bedroom. She asked me to make a braided rug for her so that she wouldn't have to step out of her bed onto a cold floor. When I asked what colors she wanted, she said she would like the rug to match the walls and bedding, and that the rug should be about 6 feet to fit in the space. For colors, she decided on slate blue, a lighter blue to match her quilt and wall trim, a mixture of grays to match the walls and chrome bed frame, and then some black, just because she wanted it. I had never made a round rug and wanted to try one for fun, and when I suggested it, she agreed to that shape. We found a wool blanket in a flea market the perfect weight and color for the lighter blue. June, one of the members of our guild, had some slate blue wool for sale that we bought, and the rest of the wool was found in the guild's stash. I had to make two trips to the stash as the rug got bigger and bigger and needed more and more wool. Luckily a friend also donated some wool to my cause. I didn't realize how much wool it actually took to do the outer rows. Those outside accent rows are butted braids with a nine-strand braid sandwiched between the three-strand braids. In the end, I had to apologize to my daughter, as the rug turned out to be only 5 feet 8 inches around.

A Festive Strip Rug

Robbie Mallin, one of our original Rocky Mountain Guild members, created this festive hit-or-miss strip rug and braided basket.

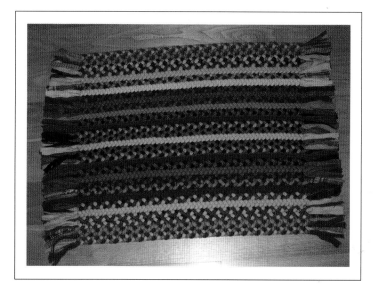

Tapis Salon

Promoting Traditional Rug Braiding in Canada

Danielle Potvin is actively promoting the revival of braided rugs in Canada. She braids, lectures, demonstrates, and teaches, using cotton in a multi-strand technique. She is president and a founding member of Guilde du Tapis Traditionnel de l'Outaouais, which is a non- profit organization dedicated to the promotion of all traditional rug making.

Victorian Christmas at Bytown Museum, Ottawa, Canada

Tyler's Bear

With much love, Sandra Meissner designed and hooked this 36 x 24-inch (91.4 x 61 cm) rug for her little grandson Tyler. As you can see, she incorporated a little braided rug into the larger, hooked rug.

Exchanging Rugs at a Summer Retreat

Danielle Potvin and Janice Watson exchange rugs at a Canadian/American rug exchange as part of a summer retreat organized by the Rocky Mountain Rug Braiders Guild.

Janice Watson, a founding member of the Rocky Mountain Rug Braider's Guild designed this large 5-foot (1.5 m) circle rug for her daughter. Over the years she has made many rugs for friends and family.

Beverly Sullivan

Beverly Sullivan is a longtime, enthusiastic member of the Rocky Mountain Rug Braider's Guild. She made this beautiful rose and green circle rug to complement her living room furnishings.

Beverly has played Mrs. Santa Claus for many years at our local Cherry Creek Mall. One of her braided rugs is usually placed in front of Santa's chair where it helps to set the spirit of Christmas and greets the thousands of little children who come each year to tell Santa their Christmas wishes. One year, Santa Claus, also known to us all as Thomas McAndrews, had a Christmas wish of his own–a request for a braided rug. Much to his delight, "Mrs. Claus" gifted him with this perfect red and green Christmas rug.

Geometry Meets Braiding

Anna Wilks fell in love with all things braided in 1997. Since that time, she has braided with every type of fabric imaginable. She says, "Give me a scrap bag and I'm a happy braider." This black, gray, and white geometric-looking rug was made by braiding six strands and finished with a hand-sewn dark gray wool binding.

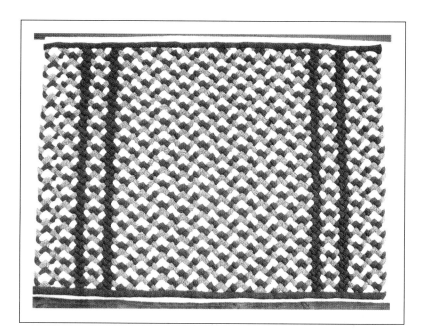

Never Too Busy to Braid

Loretta Zvarick is a lifelong braider, teacher, and mother of 12 children and three foster children. She keeps a photo of her children seated on a braided rug in her wool room to show customers that they, too, can braid with little kids around! For the past six years, she has devoted herself to building up a stock of thousands of yards of braiding material in 700 colors. Her colorful rug shown here is 6 feet (1.8 m) round.

Flower Garden Inspiration

Brian Taylor was inspired to look into braiding after seeing a small braided rug for sale that was tied to the back window of an Amish woman's horse-drawn buggy. He made this large and colorful 8 x 10-foot (2.4 x 3 m) rug for his log cabin home, using 46 wool coats.

Why Do People Braid?

People braid primarily to create a rug for a certain person or place. A homemade rug adds interest, sparkle, and warmth to a room. Children's books, television programs, and consumer magazines have kept the mystique of the braided rug alive by using them to denote comfort, home, and family. In Tasha Tudor's book, *The Dolls' Christmas*, the illustrator shows braided rugs in and in front of the dollhouse, under the childrens' Christmas tree, in the kitchen, under the cat in front of the living room fireplace, and next to the bed. In Mickey Mouse's house at Disney World, there is a braided rug in every room. Braided rugs are used occasionally in Norman Rockwell's paintings, in Disney's Peter Pan and Wendy books, and on the cover of the *Mormon Family Home Evening*. Grandma Moses used braided rugs in her illustrations for *The Night Before Christmas*, by Clement C. Moore.

One of my favorites uses of the braided rug in popular American art is a Maxwell Mays print of an old-fashioned kitchen, complete with three braided rugs and braided chair seats; it truly denotes a cheerful, happy kitchen.

One mother of seven with three dating teenage girls set her braiding table up in the living room, in direct view of the front door. As young escorts arrived, she would be found busily braiding. And, as rugs do take a long time to make, it was quite natural that she would be there once again upon the girls' return, opening up the opportunity to learn the news of the night, all without seeming to hover.

We like the idea of coming home to warm, comfortable, meaningful furnishings: heirlooms, collections, quilts, and rugs made or collected by family members. These items are like icons that connect us with the values of the past; they're part of our roots.

My daughter Bets gave me a card saying, "happiness is home-made," our family motto.

So, why do people braid? I ask my students why they are learning to braid at the start of a new class. Here are some of their answers.

-They saw a rug or a demonstrator or an article that inspired them to try it.

-Their mother, father, or grandmother braided and they know the rugs last forever.

-They like to try a lot of crafts.

-They like "country."

-They collect antiques and think braided rugs go well with them.

-They have admired friends' or neighbors' braided rugs.

-It's a relaxing craft, good for stress relief.

-They like pioneer crafts.

-They have hardwood floors and want a rug for a certain place.

-One student bought a commercial rug for her son's bedroom. He is now one year old, and the rug is wearing out. Now she's braiding one that will last.

-A dental hygienist with two children and expecting another said, to my surprise, that she wanted something to do while waiting.

-Another student priced a braided rug and decided she was too "tight" to pay the price.

-A nurse who worked in a teen psychiatric center at night liked to braid during the long night hours.

-One student's uncle was an alcoholic and took up braiding when he quit drinking.

-Several students are braiding to decorate family cabins and ranch houses.

-Many make rugs for their own homes, then go on to fill requests from relatives and friends.

-They inherited their mother's wool and want to learn to braid, too. One woman called her first rug "My Turn."

So why do I braid? After making rugs for many years for our old colonial, then for family and friends, I now braid to see the great effects obtained by combining colors. I also enjoy the challenge of making rugs with more interesting shapes.

If you fit into any of these categories or have reasons of your own and are ready to go— let's get to it!

Author at Beaver Creek, Colorado's annual folk art festival

Planning Your Rug

▼ ▼ ▼

The first thing you need to identify is the meaning behind the rug. Is it for a cozy nursery, family country kitchen, reading nook, first impression in the entryway, or is it a gift? You then interpret the desired image into decisions about size, color, and style.

Those decisions are primarily based on where you're going to put the rug. Is it a hard-use area like in front of the kitchen sink, under the table, or in an entryway? If so, you need to be sure to use sturdy wool of medium to dark colors so that your rug will wear well and resist soil. If your goal is to create a rug for a light traffic area such as a bedroom, you can use pastels and white wool.

Do you want the rug to dominate the space or blend in? Use strong colors if you want it to be a focal point; solid colors tend to look brighter. If you want it to blend into the room, use subtle colors, gradual shading, and many strands of blender colors—grays, browns, camel, beige, and tweeds in every row. Blenders tend to soften the look of the rug. If you're not sure where the rug is going to be placed, just braid in colors you like or colors you wear and you will find a place for it.

My students usually make what I call "decorator rugs." They bring beautiful swatches of upholstery fabric, drapery material, or wallpaper to match to the wool. This shows us what their color needs are.

Planning the Size of Your Rug

The second reason for knowing where you plan on putting the rug is so you can measure the area and braid an appropriate size rug. The eventual size of the rug is governed by the length of your center row.

How do you get the right size if you are making an oval rug? The rule is *measure your space, subtract the width from the length, and add one inch for every foot.*

Here's an example: The space is 4 feet wide and 5 feet long (1.2 x 1.5 m). Subtract: 5 minus 4 = 1 foot plus 1 inch. The center braid needs to be 13 inches (33.5 cm) long. You calculate every size oval rug this same way. Here's a second example: You want a 9-by-12-foot (2.8 x 3.7 m) rug. Subtract: 12 minus 9 = 3 feet (92.5 cm) plus 3 inches (8 cm). The center braid needs to be 3 feet (92.5 cm), 3 inches (8 cm) long, or 39 inches (100 cm).

Planning the size of a circle rug is even easier. You start by braiding six *twice overs* (see the circle rug directions on page 61) and continue braiding until the rug is the right size.

I recommend starting small so you can get your technique under control. The 2-by-3-foot (62 x 92.5 cm) oval rug on page 42 is specifically designed for beginners.

Planning the Type of Rug

Beginner Level Rugs

Beginners should keep their color plans simple; don't use a great many color changes, unless you are making a hit-or-miss rug. This is so you will concentrate on your braiding and lacing. First make a flat, well-shaped rug and then get more creative on your next rug.

The easiest type of rug to make is to braid any one wool plaid in pleasing colors and use the wool for all three strands. This works well for a chair seat but may be a bit monotonous for a whole rug.

Hit-or-miss rugs are also easy. There are several types:

1. Add any color wool at any time.

2. Select wools that are predominately shades of one color, as in my "Bits 'N Pieces" rug on page 87.

3. Carry one color in one strand throughout the rug. Use a second color for the second strand throughout the rug and randomly vary the color in the third strand.

4. Another easy plan is almost the same as the one above. Continue with one color per strand for two of your strands and vary the third. The difference is that instead of randomly changing the color in your third strand, you always change the color on the shoulder (as per oval directions, page 50). Coordinate your colors.

My "Bittersweet" rug on page 78 is an example of an easy-to-plan, standard shaded, 2-by-3-foot (62 x 92.5 cm) rug. It is comprised of five center rows of medium shades of wool, followed by three rows of lighter colored wool. These center colors are used again, then are gradually shaded into a darker border. To avoid having obvious color changes, you should change only one color at a time and change the color on the shoulder (see oval rug directions, page 50).

For the Advanced Braider

As an advanced braider, any number of color changes are fine. My "Country Heart" on page 68 used 15 different colors and shades of wool. If you want to change all three colors at the same time, you need to utilize the *butting* technique (page

54). In order to butt, you need to *rattail* your *continuous braid*, and then start a new braid that you butt or join together. By doing this you can change from solid red to solid blue as in my "Americana" rug, page 80.

One basic color rule: Don't place your darkest rows in the center or the rug will appear to have a hole in the center. Start your center with medium or light rows. If you start with medium- colored wools, you can shade lighter or darker. To shade lighter, take out your darkest wool strip and add a lighter strip. To shade darker, take out your lightest shade of wool and add a darker strip. Thereafter, alternate between the dark and the light bands.

I usually finish my rugs with a few rows of fairly dark wool. This frames the rug. If you like, though, you can end with medium or light rows; this tends to make your rug flow into the room. My "Victorian" rug on page 85 is one example of this look.

In my early days of rug braiding, I made monochromatic rugs. Monochromatic rugs always create a peaceful, blended look, and they are easy to design. One of our bedrooms was blue, so I made a predominately blue and grey rug. In the gold bedroom, I used many shades of gold, camel, beige, and rust (below). The rose bedroom rug is pictured on page 18. As you can see, I combined dusty rose, pink, camel, and gray. Two of my three early rugs have survived 30-something years of wear in "hard use" bedrooms. In our bedroom, we had green, blue, and gold wallpaper, so I became more adventurous and combined the three colors.

Students tend to make rugs that duplicate their teacher's "look." I try to encourage individuality and creativity, but this usually takes the experience of making a few rugs. It has always seemed harder to me to mix a lot of colors. When creating the "Nursery" rug, I bought a Beatrix Potter set of books and a lamp with Peter Rabbit in the briar patch and carefully studied the colors. My motto was if it's in the lamp, I can put it in the rug. On page 86, you can see how many colors I incorporated.

For the "Nantucket" rug (page 88), I did the same thing—found a picture and duplicated the colors. For the "Amish" and "Country Spring Heart" rugs (page 79 and page 81), I followed colors from quilts. My "Coals on the Hearth" rug (page 84) came about because I bought three long, heavy-weight wool skirts at a garage sale. I looked at the red, gray, black, and white plaids and thought they would make an interesting rug.

There are many good looking rugs in magazines and books that you can use for inspiration. If you like the rug, you can figure out approximately the color choices necessary to get the same look.Many times beginners can't translate their ideas into a color plan without a model to go by. The joy of braiding is in creating individual rugs. You need to enjoy the colors you are working with and the style you have chosen. It is only through trial and error that you will be able to judge what works for you.

Author's *Old Gold* rug, designed to match her daughter's bedroom

Wool Talk

Wool truly is the premium clothing fiber of all time, unmatched by today's man-made fibers.

Rug braiders have recognized wool's great qualities since the first braided rugs were made. Woolen rugs are soil resistant; vacuuming is all they usually need. They last almost a lifetime even in a hard-use area. My 2-x-3-foot (62 x 92.5 cm) rug in front of the door from the garage is holding up better than the wall-to-wall carpet it sits on. My front hall braided rug has stood proudly for over ten years in that demanding place.

Wool is water repellent. When I wash wool in the washing machine, I have to push it down with a long wooden spoon to get it to absorb the water. Rug braiders also appreciate the fact that wool dyes beautifully, is flame resistant, and has great bulk.

Here are answers to the most commonly asked questions I hear about wool.

What is the best weight rug wool?

I recommend wool that is easiest to braid and wears the longest. One test is to fold the edges of a 1-1/2-inch-wide (4 cm) strip into the center and then fold the edges together again: does the strip make a nice, well-rounded tube?

Braiders often buy wool by the pound. Wool that weighs between 1 pound (454 grams) and 1-3/4 pounds (794 grams) per yard is preferable. If you don't have a scale handy, the best wool includes medium-weight coat wool, medium-weight blanket wool, and heavy-weight skirt material. Wool blends are fine as long as the weight is good. Sources for purchasing rug wool are listed on pages 126–127.

Why is the weight of the wool important?

Lightweight wool produces a rug with tweaks and folds in it. This results in a unattractive rug and one that is not totally reversible. You have to cut/rip lightweight wool into 2 or 3-inch-wide (5 or 7.5 cm) strips; this means extra folding which is more time consuming; it also doesn't wear as well.

On the other hand, heavy, stiff, or flat wool, like military uniforms, Melton cloth, heavy bonded wool, and heavy blankets, is generally hard to work with. It doesn't fold easily, is hard on the hands, and makes a larger braid. Men's worsted suiting is too lightweight and flat. Loosely woven tweeds need to be cut, won't wear well, and get caught in the Braid-Aids.

Why shouldn't I recycle old wool clothes?

If you are a beginner braider, resist the temptation to use every piece of wool you have. I know that our grandmothers did this, but I believe our tastes in decorating are not the same. Many rug books extol the virtues of using any old wool garment you own or see in thrift stores, but I have only had a couple of students interested in making rugs from used clothing.

My students have found that it takes longer to make a rug when they have to take apart the garment. Moreover, it takes a lot of practice to successfully work with the differing weights of wool recycled from a cashmere coat or plaid skirt.

I suggest that you start with wool that is easy to work with—60-inch-wide (152.4 cm), clean, new, ready to use wool. You then measure 1-1/2 inches (4 cm), snip, and rip from selvage to selvage to get a 60-inch-long (152.4 cm) strip ready to braid. This is a big time saver. Coat-weight wool usually has a fuzzy and a flat side. I almost always use the flat side, but this is just a personal choice. Using the fuzzy side makes the braid look larger. Helen Howard Feeley who wrote the 1957 classic, *The Complete Book of Rug Braiding*, preferred the fuzzy side.

Gauging the weight of wool is often hard for beginners. The solution is to braid practice strips. This will help you recognize when your braid is getting larger or smaller. As you get more proficient in your braiding, you can work comfortably with varying weights of wool by varying the width of your strip.

Should I precut or prerip the wool?

No. I know it is a temptation. It looks neat to have it all ready to braid. But every time you change colors and sew on a new piece of wool, the added strip has to make the same width braid. If all of your strips are precut, you don't have this option and this might limit your color choices.

What is a good width braid?

Measure from the top dent to the bottom of the loop. My braids are usually 7/8 inches (2.2 cm) wide. A few people braid 3/4 inch (2 cm) to produce a small braid. Years ago, many rug makers braided a larger braid—up to 2 inches (5.5 cm) wide. It just depends on the look you want; it is a personal choice. The wider your braid, the more wool you use. With a wide braid, you have a heavier, thicker rug, and it braids up faster.

Some people think the larger braid looks more "country." Perhaps they do go well in rustic homes or ranches. I like "country" but I also have always made the smaller braid.

How much wool will you need?

A good rule of thumb is 2/3 pounds per square foot of rug; a 2-by-3-foot rug is 6 square feet times 2/3 = about 4 pounds of wool. The metric version of this formula is the area of the rug in square meters x 3.2 = the approximate weight of wool in kilos.

How do I take care of my rug?

This is often one of the first questions I'm asked. How would I clean it? I have only had one rug professionally dry cleaned. It is a possibility. Because wool is soil resistant, a thorough vacuuming takes care of dirt for the life of the rug. It is a good idea to turn your rugs over and around and also to use a rubberized mat or pad under the rug. This adds to the life of the rug. It is especially important to use a pad under a small rug so that it doesn't slip.

The American Wool Council has these recommendations for spot and stain removal:

Alcohol or food—place a towel under the area. Gently rub carbonated water toward the center of the spot over the stain.

Blood—blot with common starch paste and rinse from the back with soapy water.

Burning cigarette—brush off ash.

Butter and grease—sponge with a dry-cleaning solvent.

Chewing gum—scrape and sponge with a dry-cleaning solvent.

Chocolate—sponge with soapy water.

Coffee and tea—sponge with glycerine. If none is available, use warm water.

Egg—scrape and sponge with soapy water.

Glue—sponge with alcohol

Ink—immerse in cold water.

Iodine—treat with cool water followed by alcohol.

Iron rust—sponge with a weak solution of oxalic acid until the stain disappears. Then, sponge carefully with household ammonia and rinse with water.

Lipstick—may often be erased by rubbing white bread over the area with a firm, gentle motion.

Mud—once dry, brush and sponge from the back with soapy water.

Tar and road oil—sponge with dry-cleaning solvent.

Wine, Red—immerse in cold water.

This list enumerates major problems. I also use carpet spot remover. I take a toothbrush and brush the spot remover onto the stain; then I rinse well with cold water.

Cleaning with Water and Fresh Air

Usually the only problem with my braided rugs is an accumulation of soil from years of wear. If the rug needs an overall cleaning, or if there has been a recent accident, we put it on our porch chaise or picnic table and sponge with a mild liquid detergent. Then I turn the hose on to rinse the rug and let it dry outdoors. Once, we put a rug on our round picnic table to dry and the squirrels pulled up a couple of loops, so beware of squirrels.

The author's grandson, Nick Kupko, rinses a rug in the family's backyard.

Cleaning with Snow

For years I have heard people refer to cleaning their braided rugs in the snow. Judy Borger of Pottstown, Pennsylvania, described the process so clearly that I tried it and was very pleased with the results. According to Judy, you need two or more inches (5 cm) of powdery snow. Roll the rug out on an untrampled area and stomp on all parts of the rug to pack the snow into every crack underneath. Turn the rug over onto another pristine snow area and sweep off the top of the rug (the swept snow should be dirty). Then stomp on all parts of the newly swept side. Continue turning, sweeping, and stomping until the swept snow is pure white. Judy says that the rug should not be wet if the snow is powdery, and can be put right back on the floor. I hung mine for a day to be sure it was completely dry.

Trish Altman from Jericho, Vermont, cleans her rug, using the snow-cleaning method.

Cleaning with Steam Vacuums

Since *The Braided Rug Book* was first published, steam vacuums have become popular. Many people prefer to clean their own rugs rather than sending them to a dry cleaner because they have control of the process. Nancy Young has written about people having great results, using the steam vacuum on braided rugs. Loretta Zvarick recommends using the machine outside on a sunny day, on a clean surface. This way you can clean the rug, let it dry for a while, turn it over, and clean the other side.

Cleaning with Commercial Washing Machines

Another method we use now is washing in a commercial washing machine. Use caution if the rug has red wool in it, or any strong color, because it could bleed. Run the machine on the gentle cycle, using cool water; then hang to dry. Note: if you have any doubts whatsoever about whether a deep color might bleed, you can test wash a bit of wool scraps, or better yet, to be on the safe side, use another method to clean the rug.

So now we have a lot to talk about whenever we're asked how to clean a braided rug.

Braided Rugs Are Meant For Floors

Rugs love to be on the floor; they thrive and survive. They don't hold up well if rolled up and left in dark places, especially if they have been used and not cleaned thoroughly before being put away. Moths and bugs get at them and chew away. A good moth spray helps if you are storing your rugs. Also, moth balls help preserve your wool.

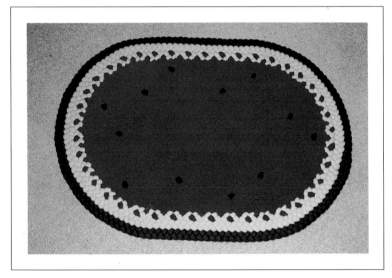

Left: Author's *Watermelon*, made from an old wool coat

Right: Jeanie Eastwood of Durango, Colorado, braided this attractive, butted denim rug, using one strand of bright multicolored wool in three of the rows.

What if I really want to recycle old wool?

Here are some tips if you can't resist taking wool clothing apart. I rip every seam, but I cut out the collar and hard-to-rip parts. These parts are usually too small to use anyway. After the garment is completely apart, I wash the pieces in the washing machine with cold water on the wool setting, using a little detergent made for washing wool. Then, I hang the pieces to dry. If hems and seams need ironing, use the wool setting and a pressing cloth. If your wool is lightweight or flat and needs to be made bulkier, try hot water and dry it in the dryer. Be careful of tweeds; wash them more gently (shorter cycle) or they will fray.

Be very selective in the clothing you take apart; for example, I never buy a bonded wool garment. Before you buy the garment or take apart your mother's old coat, ask yourself: Does it have a lot of seams? Is there a sewn-in belt? These things will shorten your strips and you will have a lot of waste.

I had two 1960s pleated skirts that looked almost the same; they weren't. One had three pieces including the skirt band and 11 ounces of usable wool. The other had 10 pieces, totaling 9 ounces of wool, and of course, a lot of wasted time and wool.

What other fabrics can I braid with?

People always ask about braiding with cotton. The technique is the same except you rip your strips wider. Making cotton rugs is not a satisfying craft for me. Cotton makes a firm, hard braid that is full of creases and tweaks; you are always battling the loose threads. Quilted cotton works okay; your bulk is sewn in. If you want to use cotton, I recommend that you crochet a rug.

Any fabric that has the same bulk or body as wool can be braided. One student was allergic to wool and made a good, colorful rug out of velour. Another student, Judith Felsburg, made a terrific rug out of denim to match her son's bedroom.

I started this chapter by saying that wool lasts almost forever. Take my watermelon rug for example. After searching for the right shade, I remembered a coat I had about 50 years ago that was in a chest in the basement. As you can see, it made a great watermelon.

I don't mean to discourage you from braiding old wool; it is fun using some wool you can identify as belonging to a family member or friend. Once I was told that my "Old Sparhawk" rug was lost in shipping. My response was, "Oh no, my father's bathrobe and son's Valley Forge pants are in it!" Recycled wool does present certain technical and design challenges, and you may want to make a first rug using new wool.

Sometimes when I am demonstrating, people are surprised that one or several of the strands I am using came from coats I have taken apart. This appeals to people, especially when I demonstrate at historic places. They like the fact that we are still doing rugs the way they were done in the "olden" days.

Getting Started

▼   ▼   ▼

You are now ready to start braiding. Rug braiding, like many crafts, is accomplished by using a number of specialized and general tools. If you are new to braiding, I recommend that you acquire the following items on the list below. You'll see that compared to other crafts, braiding requires very few gadgets. If you own a basic sewing machine and can use a needle and thread, you are off to a great start!

Basic Equipment

Table to attach a braiding clamp to and to lace on

Sewing machine to attach strips

Braiding clamp

Vari-Folder Braid-Aids (optional)

Braidkin (lacing needle)

6-ply linen lacing thread (or)

Braided cotton splicing thread (or)

Beeswax nylon thread

1-1/4-inch (3.2 cm) T-pins or plastic-headed pins

6-inch (15.2 cm) metal ruler

Sharp dressmaker scissors

6 #2 safety pins

Sewing needles and matching thread

Medium-size tapestry needle, #18 or #19

Needle-nose pliers or hemostat

Loose-fitting glove with fingertips cut off for wearing on lacing hand (optional)

Rug braiding stand (optional)

General Rules for Easy Braiding

There are a few general rules to follow that really do make it easier to braid well.

First of all, find a comfortable place to braid. You will need to work at a large table. Sit in a comfortable chair and make sure you have good lighting.

Attach a clamp to the table or use a floor stand. A clamp does a good job of holding your braid while you work. Set up your sewing machine close to your work table. Although wool strips can be attached by hand, I find it quicker and the stitches tighter when I use a sewing machine. Last, but by no means least, always lace on a table or other flat surface.

Preparing Wool Strips

Prepare strips only when you are ready for them. Wool weight varies so much that it's important to have the flexibility of varying the width.

Rip the wool whenever possible. When ripping strips, use a metal ruler. Measure each strip carefully, cut a couple of inches and rip the rest. Check the width to make sure the wool is ripping straight. Tweeds sometimes need to be cut. When cutting, measure all along the wool to keep the width uniform.

When ripping or cutting wool, go from selvage to selvage or the length of the piece, whichever produces the longest strip.

My instructions say to cut or rip your strips 1-1/2 inches (4 cm) wide. This is for the best weight wool, coat weight. No two pieces of wool are the same. When you're starting a rug or changing colors, try one strip and check the look of the braid. The braid needs to remain the same width.

If you have only lighter weight wool, your strips should be anywhere from 1-3/4 inches (4.4 cm) to 2-1/2 inches (6.4 cm) wide. Lightweight wool (like skirt weight) tends to tweak. This means there are wrinkles in your braid. If possible, use only one strand of lightweight wool along with two strands of good weight wool at a time.

If you are a beginner, try to find the best weight wool so that the edges fold in easily. Advanced braiders can braid all types and weights of material.

My braids are approximately 7/8 inches (2.2 cm) wide, measuring from the dent on one side to the hump opposite it.

Basic Techniques

Instead of reading through a basic techniques section in advance of the projects, you will learn all the techniques you need as you braid a complete rug.

We'll start with the oval rug, by far the most popular braided rug shape. This is a small rug--a good beginner size. We'll meander slowly and carefully through this project, stopping often to learn in detail how to execute all the elements that go into braiding a rug.

The second project is the circle rug; instead of repeating the basic techniques, you will refer to those steps in the oval rug. This rug is slightly larger than the oval.

The third project is for making a heart-shaped rug, a more difficult undertaking. Here again, you will refer back to the oval rug at key stages.

The fourth and fifth projects—the strip rug and the five-strand rug—are advanced projects, with still fewer basic directions. You can always refer to the earlier projects to review basic techniques if needed.

Before you begin the projects, read the glossary on page 125 so that you will recognize the braiding terms. Also, read the project instructions at least twice, and try to visualize and reason through all the steps. That way, you'll be familiar with the road we're going to take.

Cat Rug Braiding Stand with Storage Box

Original design by Bill Lucas and Richard Beauvais-Niki, modified by Karen Kafka

What You Need

One 1-inch-thick (2.5 cm) piece of lumber (I used pine), 8 inches (20.3 cm) wide x 4 feet (1.22 m) long

Scrap of fiberboard, 1/4 inch (6 mm) thick

Scrap of plywood, 3/4 inch (1.9 mm) thick

Wood glue

Wood filler (optional)

Sandpaper, coarse and fine-grid

Paint, stain, or clear polyurethane

Paintbrush

2 carriage bolts, 1/4 x 2 inches (6 mm x 5.1cm) with washers and nuts

One 1/4-inch (6 mm) butterfly or wing nut

One 1/4-inch (6 mm) x 3-inch-long (7.6 cm) spring

2 decorative hinges

Latch for box top

What You Do

1. Rip a 4-inch-wide (10.2 cm) board 4 feet (1.22 m) long.

2. Crosscut from the 4-inch-wide length of board:
   Two 15-inch (38.1 cm) pieces for box sides or side-pieces
   One 9-inch (22.9 cm) piece for box top
   One 4-inch (10.2 cm) piece for box front
   One 2-5/8-inch (6.7 cm) piece for box back

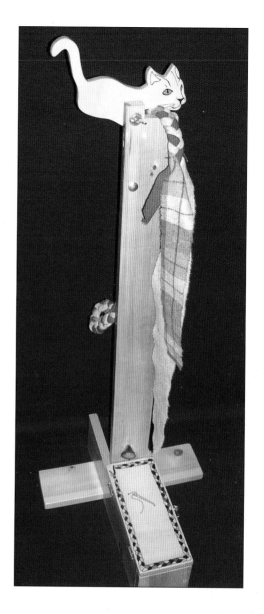

3. Crosscut from the remaining piece of board:
   One 15-inch (38.1 cm) piece for the crossbar

4. Rip that remaining board length to a 3-inch-wide (7.6 cm) board. Crosscut one 30-inch piece (76.2 cm) for the staff.

5. From the 1/4-inch-thick (6 mm) fiberboard, cut a piece 3 x 7 1/2 inches (7.6 x 19.1 cm) long for box bottom. Cut after dados to check for fit. It should extend 1/4 inch (6 mm) beyond sidepieces to insert into box-front dado.

6. Enlarge the template of the cat to 3 x 6 inches (7.6 x 15.2 cm; that's 125%. Trace the pattern onto a piece of 3/4-inch (1.9 cm) wood or plywood and cut out.

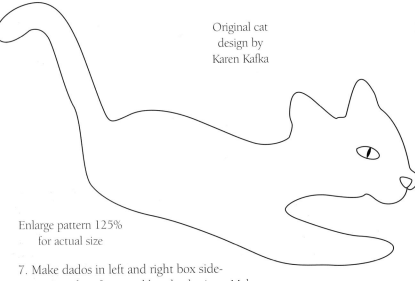

Original cat
design by
Karen Kafka

Enlarge pattern 125%
for actual size

7. Make dados in left and right box sidepieces, box front and box back piece. Make
notches in box sidepieces as shown in diagrams below.

8. Cut a 2-inch-wide (5.1 cm) x 1-inch-high (2.5 cm) notch

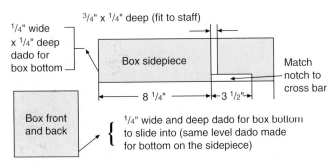

¹/₄" wide
x ¹/₄" deep
dado for
box bottom

³/₄" x ¹/₄" deep (fit to staff)

Box sidepiece

Match
notch to
cross bar

8 ¹/₄"   3 ¹/₂"

Box front
and back

¹/₄" wide and deep dado for box bottom
to slide into (same level dado made
for bottom on the sidepiece)

at the top of the 30-inch (76.2 cm) staff (photo 3). Fill
areas as needed with wood filler. Sand all pieces
smooth. Check fit of all pieces before final assembly.
The staff should fit snuggly into the vertical dados of
sidepieces.

- The box bottom should slide into the horizontal
  sidepiece dados.

- The crossbar should fit the notches on the sidepieces.

- The box should sit evenly on a level surface (photo 2).

9. Assemble box with glue, screws, and nails, or pegs.
Secure the cross-
bar to the box.

10. I like to decorate
the cat with a
face and the
box with a
design.

11. Paint, stain, or
polyurethane all
wood pieces.

Photo 2

12. Drill a 1/4-inch (6 mm) hole about 1 inch
(2.5 cm) from the tip of the cat's leg or
whale's lip for one end of the spring, or
hold spring in place with a screw. Drill a
1/4-inch (6 mm) hole 1 inch (2.5 cm)
down and 5/8 inch (1.6 cm) in on post or
extension on top of
staff, and measure
down 4-3/4 inches on
the same side of the
staff, and drill a 1/4-
inch (6 mm) hole for
bolt.

13. Attach spring. I put the
washer, nut, spring,
and nut on the bottom
hole to hold the spring
away from the wood
(photos 3 and 4).

Photo 3

14. Line up upper ledge of cat's leg or
whale's lip with the 2-inch (5.1
cm) ledge of notch made in staff.
Drill a 1/4-inch (6 mm) hole through cat or whale for
bolt and wing nut (photo 4).

When the wing nut is
loosened and the tail is
pushed down, the braid
releases and can be
moved; when the tail is
released, the spring cre-
ates tension on the
braid, is held in place
by the tightened wing
nut, and secures the
braid for braiding.
(Note: Place the tail on
the left side for right-
handed persons; tail on the right side for left-handed persons. Photo shows tail for right-handed person.) The spring
will be on the side of the staff away from the braider.

Photo 4

I lined the bottom of the supply box with adhesive felt.
Attach the hinges and the latch to the box top and sidepieces. Since I'm right-handed, I put the latch on the right-
hand side. I put the box between my feet and under my
chair when I braid. Adjust the location of the latch to your
placement preference. Put supplies in the box. My box holds
braid-aids, needles, pins, thread, tape measure, hemostats,
etc. I also made a tapestry bag that carries the stand, the
rug, and pieces of rug wool to those wonderful rug-braiding
activities.

Portable Rug Braiding Stand

Designed and made by Karen Kafka

Take your portable rug stand with you to all those wonderful rug-braiding retreats around the country. It's only 18 inches long and 10 inches wide and weighs a mere 3 pounds, even with the hardware, and even less than that if the wood is secured with screws or pegs.

What You Need

Pieces of wood:

Two 1 x 2 1/2 x 17 1/2 inches (2.5 x 6.4 x 44.5 cm) long for staff

Two 1 x 2 1/2 x 3 inches (2.5 x 6.4 x 7.66 cm) long for top

Two 3/4 x 1 1/2 x 3 inches (1.9 x 3.8 x 7.6 cm) long for side stabilizers (pre-drill when nailing to prevent splitting)

Wood for top, if making the interchangeable units (photo 5).

Two 1 x 2 5/8 x 6 3/4 inches (2.5 x 6.7 x 17.1 cm) long for base

Two 1 x 2 5/8 x 8 3/4 inches (2.5 x 6.7 x 22.2 cm) long for base (base designed by Ken Kafka; I cut a nice curving shape.)

Wood glue, wood filler, coarse and fine-grit sandpaper

Paint, stain, or clear polyurethane finish and paintbrush

Two carriage bolts, 1/4 x 2 1/2 inches (6mm x 6.4 cm) long for top

One carriage bolt, 1/4 x 2 inches (6 mm x 5.1 cm) long for staff with washers and nuts (I like wing nuts.)

One heavy-duty 1/4 x 1 1/4-inch-diameter (6mm x 5.1 cm) washer

What You Do

1. Sand all pieces of wood smooth.

2. On one of the 17-1/2 -inch-long (44.5 cm) pieces, make a 3/8-inch-wide (9.5 cm) mortis, starting 1 3/4 inch (4.4 cm) from the end and ending 4 1/2 inches (11.4 cm) from the other end. The mortis allows the stand's height to adjust to 30 inches (76.2 cm) (photo 2).

Photo 2

3. On the other 17-1/2-inch-long (44.5 cm) piece, measure 2 inches (5.1 cm) from the end and drill a 1/4-inch (6 mm) hole to insert the 2-inch (5.1 cm) carriage bolt through the hole. Secure the 3/4 x 1-1/2-inch (1.9 x 3.8 cm) side stabilizers to the staff, centered to the drilled 1/4-inch (6 mm) hole, or use two bolts 2 (5.1 cm) inches apart (photo 3).

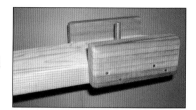

Photo 3

4. Assemble the base to fit the staff (photo 4). The longer boards go toward and away from you. The shorter boards are pointing out to the side. The assembled base can be one unit or bolted with the staff sandwiched between the base units.

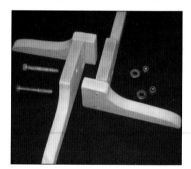

Photo 4

5. If you just want one kind of unit, secure the top pieces or drill 1/4-inch (6 mm) holes through the two 1 x 2 1/2 x 3-inch (2.5 x 6.4 x 7.6 cm) top pieces and the end of the mortised piece for unit interchanges between a three-strand unit and a multi-strand unit. Rug hookers have a metal strip to hold the rug; works well for braids. I stapled the metal hooking strip to the piece of wood crossing the top (photo 5).

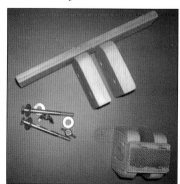

Photo 5

6. Wood-fill areas as needed, finish sanding, and paint, stain or polyurethane to finish.

The Oval Braided Rug

▼ ▼ ▼

The oval rug is one of the easiest to make. It is the most popular shape, probably because it fits a great many areas. My "Country Spring Oval" (below) is 2 by 3 feet (61.5 x 92.5 cm), a good size for the beginner braider.

Calculating the Length of the First Row

To figure out the length of the first row, subtract the 2 foot width (61.5 cm) from the 3 foot (92.5 cm) length. This gives you 1 foot (31 cm). Add 1 inch (2 cm): the center braid is 13 inches (33 cm) long.

This is a standard design, going from medium shades in the center to darker bands, then some light, and ending with the darkest bands. Beginners may not want to include as many colors. Yellow, purple, and green could be eliminated and the look would be almost the same. This would leave six colors, a good number for the novice braider. Light gray could be substituted for white, making the rug more soil resistant.

How to Count Rows

Basic to braiding is knowing how to count rows. Here's how it's done:

The first 13 inches (33 cm)—or the distance to the twice overs—is Row 1. Row 2 is all the way around the center row. Row 3 and the following rows are a complete circuit of the rug.

Materials

The "Country Spring Oval" uses about 4-1/2 pounds (2.1 kilos) of wool, or 4 yards (3.7 m). Review the equipment listed on page 38. Make sure you have matching sewing thread.

Country Spring Oval

Rows 1-3	White	Med. Blue	Lt. Blue
Row 4	Dusty Rose	Med. Blue	Lt. Blue
Rows 5 & 6	Dusty Rose	Med. Blue	Blue Gray
Row 7	Dusty Rose	Med. Purple	Blue Gray
Row 8	Dusty Rose	Med. Purple	White
Row 9	Lt. Pink	Med. Purple	White
Row 10	Lt. Pink	Lt. Yellow	White
Row 11	Lt. Pink	Lt. Blue	White
Row 12	Med. Blue	Lt. Blue	White
Row 13	Med. Blue	Lt. Blue	Med. Green
Row 14	Med. Blue	Blue Gray	Med. Green
Row 15	Med. Blue	Dusty Rose	Dusty Rose
Row 16	Dusty Rose	Dusty Rose	Dusty Rose

Illustrations

Figure 1 diagrams all the key elements of the oval rug. You will refer to this illustration a number of times as you follow the instructions. In all the illustrations, black, white, and gray indicate different colors of wool.

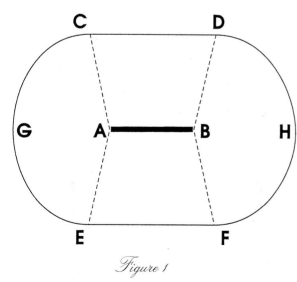

Figure 1

A - "T" Beginning
B - 2-Twice overs
C - D and E - F - No skip areas
D - F and E - C - Skipping Areas
B to F - Color change area
F - Rattail area
G - Butt here for 1st butted row
H - Butt here on last row

T-start

All braided rugs begin with a *T-start*.

1. Cut or rip one strand each of your chosen colors 1-1/2 inches (4 cm) wide. If the selvage is bulky, cut it off.

2. Put the right side of one strip facing up.

Tip Some wool looks alike on both sides. Other wool has a flat side, which I call the right side, and a fuzzy side, called the wrong side. Other braiders like to use the fuzzy side as the right side. Whichever you choose, be consistent. Always sew the right sides of the wool together.

1. Put the right side of a second strip at right angles on the end of the first strip (right side down). In other words, place the right sides together (figure 2).

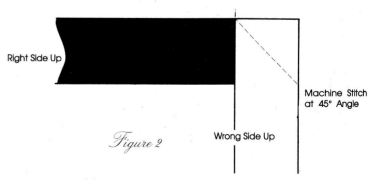

Figure 2

2. Machine stitch from the top left corner to the side, using matching thread (figure 2). Trim close to the stitching, leaving approximately 1/8 inch (.5 cm) as shown in figure 3.

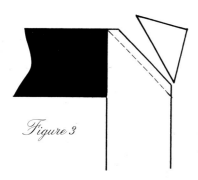

Figure 3

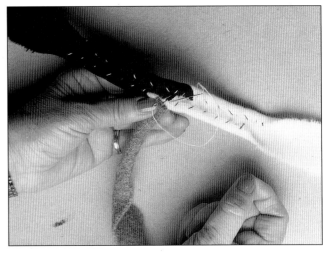

3. Working on the wrong side of the combined strips, turn in 1/4 inch (1 cm) on both sides of the diagonal seam for 2 to 3 inches (5 to 7.5 cm); pin to hold. Overcast both the top and bottom, using matching sewing thread (figure 4). The stitches should not show on the right side.

4. Take a third strip and fold the edges into the center. Fold again to the center and blind stitch the edge for 2 to 3 inches (5 to 7.5 cm), using matching thread (figure 5).

5. Sew this tube firmly to the center on the lower seam. Position the folded edges to the left (figure 6).

Attaching the third strip to the center

6. Fold the top half of the combined strips over the bottom half and blind stitch 2 to 3 inches (5 to 7.5 cm) on both sides of the center seam, enclosing the tube (figure 7). You have now completed the *T*.

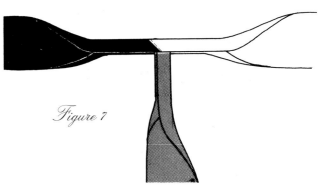

Figure 4

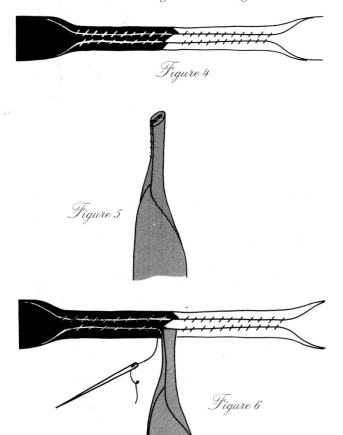

Figure 5

Figure 6

Figure 7

7. If you are using Braid-Aids, attach them to all three strips (see the photograph below).

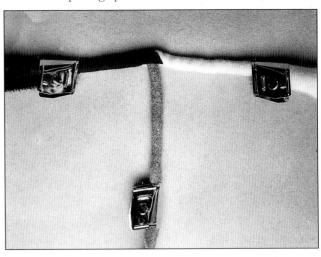

Braid-Aids in place on completed *T*

Braiding

1. Roll up one strand of wool to 2 feet (61.5 cm) from the *T* and pin. Keeping one strand shorter or rolled up throughout the braiding process keeps the three strands from tangling.

2. Hold the *T* so that the third tube has the fold on the left. Fold the edges in by hand or use Braid-Aids to fold.

3. Pull the right tube *over* the center tube and hold (figure 8). *Always keep the folds on the left.*

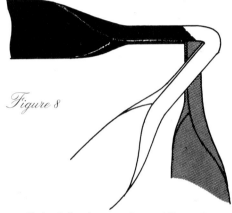

Figure 8

4. Now pull the left tube *over* the middle to the center and twist so the fold is on the left (figure 9). Hold with your left hand.

Figure 9

5. Continue braiding. Fold the edges in, take from the right, put the tube in the center and hold with the right hand. Now fold the edges in on the strand on the left, pull tightly to the center, and hold with the left hand. Make sure your folds are on the left. Check the other side of the braid to make sure that the folds aren't showing.

6. Put a large safety pin through the loops to hold the braid together when you stop.

7. Braid for 2 inches (5 cm) and put the braid into the clamp. Always keep some tension on your clamp. Pull as you're braiding (see photographs opposite).

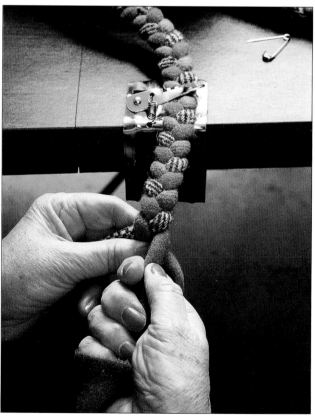

8. Braid for 13 inches (33 cm), and then braid two *twice overs*.
   a. Take a tube on the right and braid (figure 10a).
   b. Take the next tube from the *right*, braid and hold (figure 10b).
   c. Braid the tube from the left and pull *tightly* (figure 10c).
   d. Repeat a, b, and c once more (figure 11).

This is the only time a corner is braided in.

9. Braid about 36 inches (92.5 cm). When you attach your strips, place the right sides together as per figure 2 and trim as in figure 3.

Tip You may want to take your braid out now and practice until you have an even, tight braid.

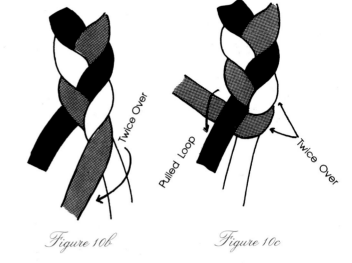

Figure 10a   *Figure 10b*   *Figure 10c*

Lacing

1. Now we're ready to *lace* or sew the braid together. Take about 5 feet (152.4 cm) of lacing thread. Thread it into the *tapestry* needle and knot.

Tip Keep the right side of the rug up; this is the side that is up when you are braiding.

2. Position the *T* away from you and to your left (figure 11).

3. Insert the needle through the wool *into* the second *pulled loop*. After braiding twice overs, the single loop on the

opposite side is pulled tightly, therefore called a pulled loop. This attaches the thread firmly and hides the knot (figure 12).

4. The lacing technique for the first 13 inches (33 cm)—the first row—is different from the rest of the rug. The reason is that the braid in these first inches (until the *T* is reached) goes in the opposite direction from the braid in the next 13 inches (33 cm).

There are two methods of lacing this first 13 inches (33 cm).

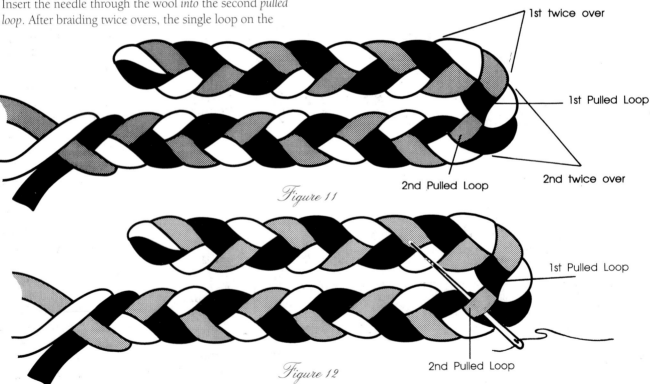

1st twice over

1st Pulled Loop

2nd Pulled Loop   2nd twice over

Figure 11

1st Pulled Loop

2nd Pulled Loop

Figure 12

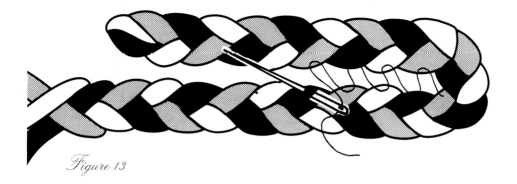

Figure 13

Method #1

Insert the tapestry needle as mentioned above and shown in figure 12. Sew each loop, alternating the sides on the fold side of the braid (figure 13). Pull the lacing thread tightly after each stitch. Continue until you reach the *T*.

This method is easy to do. The stitches are hidden, it is sewn tightly, and the loops are alternating as in the rest of the rug.

Method #2:

Method #2 is called a *reverse e* because the stitches look like an "e" going backward (figure 18). This method has been the accepted way for many years.

Figure 14

Figure 15

a. Insert the tapestry needle as in figure 12. Now switch to the *lacing needle* (the Braidkin).

b. Insert the lacing needle through the space between the next loop to the left (figure 14).

c. Cross to the upper braid, insert the needle into the opposite loop going from the left to right. Use the lacing needle to hide the thread and pull (figure 15).

d. Cross back down to the lower braid, lace in the loop already laced, going toward the left (figure 16).

e. Lace in the loop to its left (for the first time). Hide the thread and pull (figure 17). For example: Go from 1 to 2, then up to 3 (going from left to right), back to 4 again and then to 5 (figure 18).

This method is harder to learn. If you're using three strands of solid colored wool, it is a bit hard to hide your stitches. It also leaves a line down the center because your stitches aren't woven together, as in the rest of the rug.

Figure 16

It is a good idea to learn both methods as both have advantages.

The directions from here on are the same for both methods.

5. Lace until you reach the *T*.

6. Switch to the tapestry needle. Insert it through the bottom of the *T*, halfway from the bottom to the top. Take a 1/4-inch (1 cm) stitch. Skip one loop on the braid you are attaching and lace the next loop. Pull the thread. *Turn your rug as you are going around the T.*

7. Take a 1/4-inch (1 cm) stitch at the end of the *T* and skip the next loop on the row you are attaching; lace the next loop (figure 19).

8. Take one more stitch on the other side of the *T*, skip a loop on the row you're attaching (working braid), then lace the next loop.

   The *T* is now laced.

9. Return the thread to the lacing needle.

10. The following is the technique to be used for the rest of the rug.

    a. Lace only in one direction—toward your *left*.

    b. Lace through the loop to the left of the *T*, going from right to left; pull the thread.

    c. Lace the next loop in the braid you are attaching. Cross up to the body of rug and lace going from right to left. Hide the lacing thread and pull, *holding both braids flat as you pull* (figure 20).

    d. Continue lacing in this manner until you reach the curved end. *Never skip on the straight side of the rug. Lace in every loop.*

    e. Skip four times on this second curve (skip every other loop). *Skip only on the outside braid— never on the body of the rug.*

11. Continue braiding and lacing until three rows are completed.

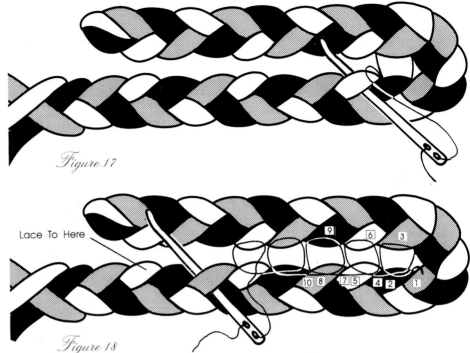

Figure 17

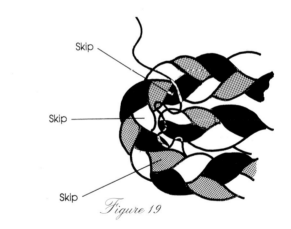

Lace To Here

Figure 18

Skip

Skip

Skip

Figure 19

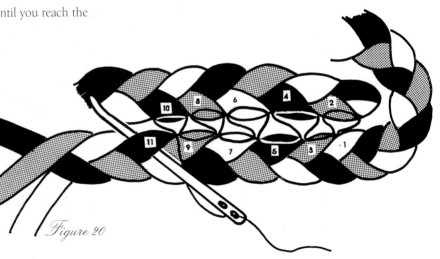

Figure 20

Tip To attach a new piece of lacing thread, use a square knot: Left over right and around; then right over left and around. Pull tightly (figure 21). Always hide the knot. Push it into the folds with the lacing needle and check the back of the rug to make sure it's completely hidden.

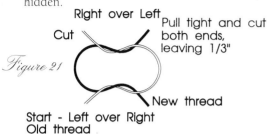

Right over Left
Pull tight and cut
both ends,
leaving 1/3"
Cut
Figure 21
New thread
Start - Left over Right
Old thread

General Rules for Lacing and Skipping

It's a good practice to braid a row and then lace it. This is the time to decide if you want to change a color. Here are some general rules for mastering lacing.

▼ Four to six skips (increases) on the curve normally will keep it flat. Space your skips evenly around the curve.

▼ Skip about the same number of times on both ends of the row.

▼ If the rug scallops, there are too many skips. If it cups up, there are not enough.

▼ Establish a routine; for example, lace three loops (on the braid you are attaching) and skip one loop all around the curve. The key is to skip evenly and alternate your skips. As the rug gets bigger, the skips get farther apart. Figure 22 diagrams the approximate placement of skips and shows where to change colors.

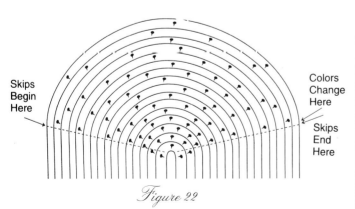

Skips
Begin
Here

Colors
Change
Here

Skips
End
Here

Figure 22

▼ It is impossible to make a hard and fast rule regarding how many skips and how often. If you have changed the width of your braid, skip less if it is wider; skip more if it is narrower.

Lacing and Skipping on the Oval Rug

▼ When lacing on the curved ends, always lace the loop on the braid you are attaching; then lace the next loop on the body of the rug. Hold flat and pull. Evaluate whether to skip the next loop on the row you are attaching. If the lacing thread is ahead of the next loop on the row you are attaching (working braid), skip it and lace the next loop. Now lace the top loop on the body of the rug (figure 23).

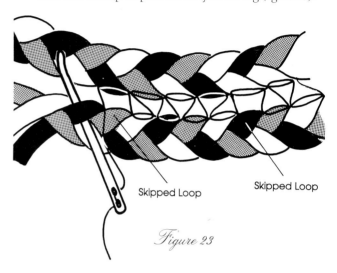

Skipped Loop   Skipped Loop

Figure 23

▼ Starting on the third row, put a T-pin in every skipped loop. Keep them in place for approximately five rows.

▼ Avoid skipping in the same place. If you place a pin where you skip, it will mark the place where you skipped in the previous rows.

▼ Mark the *T* and the twice overs with a large straight pin on A and B (figure 1). This will help you know when it is time to start thinking about starting or ending your skips.

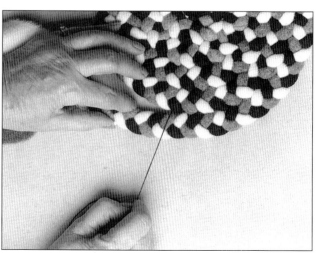

Not ready to skip

Time to skip

▼ Start skipping when the ends of the rug start forming the curve. Early or late skips will make barbells or bulges where it should be straight.

▼ Check the straight sides of your rug every row for these first two to four rows; line the side up with the edge of the table and mold the rug into a straight line. Your rug will be pliable now. If it is banana-shaped now, you won't be able to correct this later.

Tip The photographs below show regular lacing. Notice how I laced the plaid in the photograph on the left, pulling the braid open. This enables the thread to line up in the space between the loops so that the lacing thread can be hidden. The other photograph shows lacing the top loop. Hold the braids together and pull tightly to hide the lacing thread with the needle.

Changing Colors

When you change colors, you want to avoid being obvious; you want your new color to make its appearance in a subtle fashion. To change colors successfully, follow these steps:

1. Change to a new color on the opposite end of the *T* (figure 1 and figure 22).

2. Complete 3 rows (or the number of rows you would like before making a color change.)

3. Braid beyond the curve.

4. Hold a ruler along the straight side of the rug or put the rug along the side of a table.

5. The outside loop to the right of the edge is the loop to remove.

6. Put a T-pin *above* and *below* the preceding loop in the loop to be removed (figure 24).

Color To Be Removed

Figure 24

Lacing the braid you are attaching

Lacing the top loop

7. Unbraid 2 inches (5 cm) beyond the T-pins and cut between them at a 45-degree angle (figure 25).

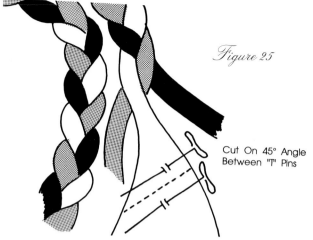

Figure 25

Cut On 45° Angle
Between "T" Pins

New color sewn on

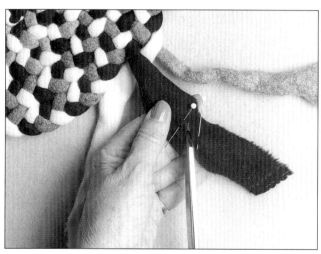

Cutting between the T-pins

Braiding with new color

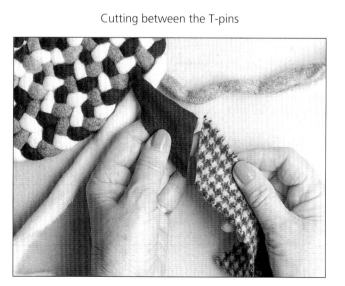

Placement of new color

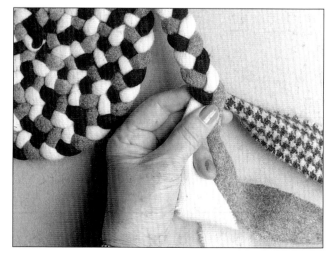

Sewn edge concealed by braid

New color appears in braid

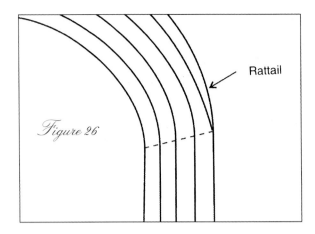

Figure 26

Rattail

8. Sew the strip of new color to the unbraided strip you just cut; sew along the cut line. Rebraid the three strands. The seam you just sewed should be under the preceding loop; the new color will be on the right side of the braid.

9. Continue braiding, lacing, and changing colors as per the color chart on page 43 until you've completed 14 rows or the number of rows you need to almost finish the rug.

10. Change only one color at a time to blend colors well.

Tip Some braiders hide their seam when attaching a new strip. This is done by having the seam fall under the loop as shown in figures 24 and 25. I recommend hiding the seam if you're using solid colors as in the "Watermelon" rug (page 36) or "Country Spring" (page 42). If your rug is tweedy, or when you use more neutral or darker colors, the seams don't show anyway. I have never found that these seams wear quickly. Tight, sewing machine stitches hold up well. If you are attaching strips by hand, it may be better to hide the seam.

Rattailing or Tapering

Rattailing or tapering is a method of ending a continuous braid. Many braiders end their rugs this way. I use rattailing at the point in the rug where I want the continuous braid to end; then I butt to finish the rug.

1. Refer to figures 1 and 26 (above, right) for areas to rattail. Put a T-pin in the braid where the curve ends. This is where the braid should end.

2. Cut off the braid 1 inch (2.5 cm) below this pin and unbraid 8 inches (20.5 cm).

3. To taper, cut all three strands so that they measure 5/8 inch (1.6 cm) on the ends; cut up both sides for 6–8 inches, gradually widening your cut until the wool is a normal width (photo below).

Strands cut to 5/8 inch (1.6 cm) on ends

4. Rebraid the rattail as far as you can, still folding the edges in. When the rattail gets so narrow that the edges can no longer be folded by hand, blind stitch the remaining edges. These ends should be as small as you can make them. Braid all but the final inch (2.5 cm) and pin to hold.

5. Lace to the last inch (2.5 cm).

Lacing the rattail to the last inch

6. Using needle-nose pliers, weave the most obvious color strand into its matching color in the rug, if possible. Pull through one loop onto the body of the rug (figure 28). Twist the remaining two loops around each other and weave the next most obvious color through the next loop in the rug. Weave the final loop in the same color loop in the rug. If this doesn't look smooth or is too obvious, try again. Sometimes you can do better using a different combination.

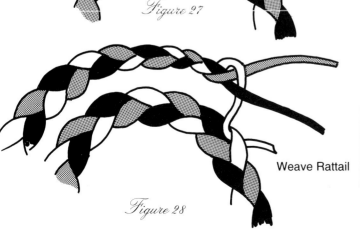

Figure 27

Weave Rattail

Figure 28

First strand ready to pull in

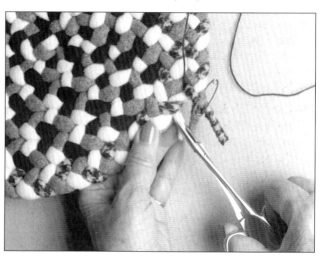

Pulling in first strand

Pulling in second strand

Pulling in third strand

7. Cut the ends of the loops (on the back of rug) even with the side of the loop it was pulled through. Take a needle and matching thread and sew to secure these ends. This completes your continuous braid.

Butting

Butting is a method of forming one complete row by weaving the two ends of a braid together to form a necklace; then you lace the necklace around the rug. All loose ends are carefully concealed. Butting seamlessly frames, and thereby finishes, the rug. I always end my rugs with one or two butted rows.

Butting is also the best technique for radically changing colors without showing a color change area; my "Americana" rug on page 80 is a good example of how that approach works.

In addition, butting protects the rattail from coming unraveled. And it is a wonderful way to add rows to large rugs and thereby avoid having to carry the whole rug to the sewing machine every time you need to add strands of wool to your continuous braid.

The last point I need to make here is that butting is the most challenging aspect of making a braided rug. In my classes, this is the technique students need the most help with. An easy way to visualize butting is to think of it as joining two ends of braid together by weaving same-colored loops through each other. Once you get the hang of it, you'll be able to butt with the best of them.

If you are butting the whole rug, or any part of it, use the following directions.

Butting - Row 15 (or your next to the last row)

1. Fold in the edges of all three strands. Pin each strand with a #2 (large) safety pin (figure 29).

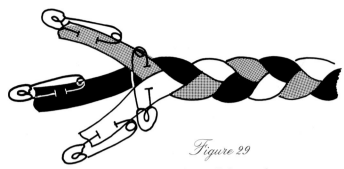

Figure 29

2. Place the folds to the left and put all three tubes into your clamp. The large pins will hold the tubes in the clamp.

Three tubes secured in clamp

3. Braid a few inches (5 or 6 cm) and put a fourth pin across all the loops (figure 29).

4. Braid until you have a length of braid long enough to go around the rug once.

Length of braid ready to butt

5. Place the ends to be butted on a curve (figure 1). Remember to place the braid clockwise (in the same direction as the rest of the rug), with the top of your braid up.

6. Leave 5-6 inches (13-15 cm) of lacing thread and start lacing 4 inches (10 cm) from the beginning of the braid.

Beginning of lacing butted rug

Beginning of row pinned over end of row

7. Lace all around the rug, leaving 4 inches (10 cm) unlaced on the end.

8. Braid enough so that you can overlap the two ends of your braid by 3-4 inches (7.5-10 cm).

9. Place the pinned end of the braid (the beginning) on top of the other end. Match the same colors: for example, place white on top of white, gray on top of gray (figure 30).

Matching colors pinned together

11. Take out any pins left on the ends and unbraid to the pinned loops. Cut the ends of the braid so that approximately 2 inches (5 cm) remain on each end of the braid.

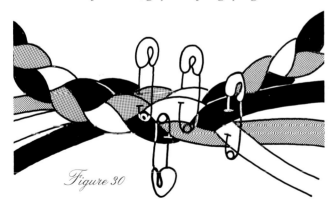

Figure 30

Tip Double-check to be sure the braid is long enough; you need to have enough braid to lace the final 8 inches (20.5 cm) to the rug without stretching the braid.

10. Pin two matching loops together on the fold side (inside); for example, pin white to white, and gray to gray. Pin the third loops (between these two) together on the outside (figure 30).

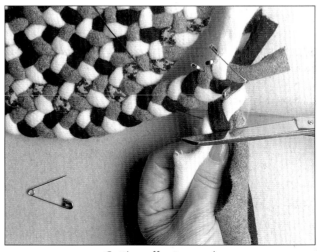

Cutting off extra wool

12. You will start to butt with the ends of one loop of each color free on the fold side. Both loops will be free on the outside (figure 31).

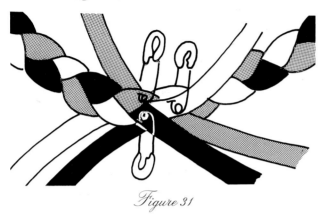

Figure 31

Tip Hold onto the butting area firmly with your left hand; don't let go. Do all of your pinning, etc., with your right hand.

Removing pins; hold firmly in left hand

13. Work with the outside loops. Cross the top loop over the bottom loop and pull out all the fullness. Make sure the edges are folded in. Unpin and repin along the side of the braid (figure 32).

Cut
Pin Along Dotted Line
Cut & Overcast
Inside
Outside
Figure 32
Cut
Pin Along Dotted Line

Repinning along edge

14. Next work on the loop to the right on the fold side. Insert the lacing needle in front of the back loop and pull the end up and out; it will be crossed behind its matching loop. Pull to tighten. Unpin and repin along the edge of the braid.

Pulling inside loop through and crossing over

Pinning lengthwise

15. Using the lacing needle, insert it in front of the front loop on the left. Pull the end out; it will cross in front of the matching loop. Pull out all the fullness. Unpin and repin along the edge of the braid. You have now woven your two ends together.

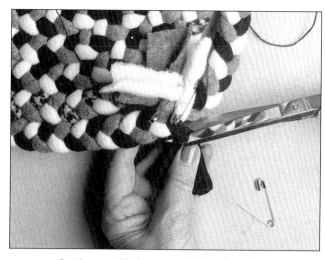

Cutting outside loop even with edge of rug

Pulling last loop through

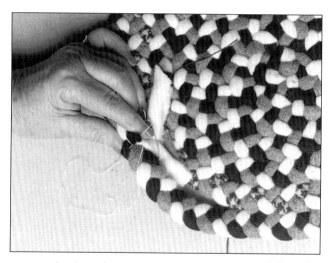

Sewing edges together even with side of rug

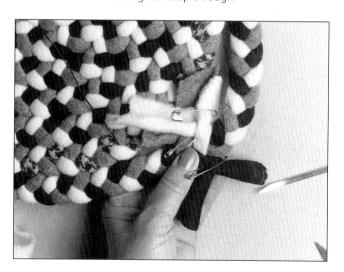

Crossing over and pinning lengthwise

16. Unpin the outside loops and cut both the front and back loops even with the edge of the braid (figure 32). Hold the cut edges together. Overcast firmly with matching thread.

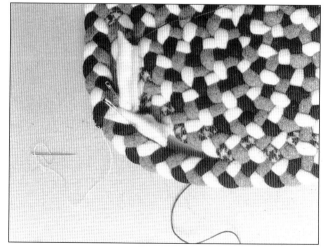

Outside edge, sewn

17. Repeat for the top loops. Cut the loops on the right even with the edge of the braid and overcast. Then cut the loops on the left even with the braid and overcast. The sewn edges should fall between the rows so the stitching doesn't show.

18. Lace the final 8 inches (20.5 cm) of braid to the rug. Weave the lacing thread through the loops until you come back to where you started to lace and tie.

All loops cut and sewn

Butting - Last Row

The instructions for the last row are a bit different—all your butting seams are on the fold side (inside). Repeat steps 1-9. Then continue with steps 19-28.

19. Pin all three loops on the inside, with one pin on the outside, just to hold (figure 33).

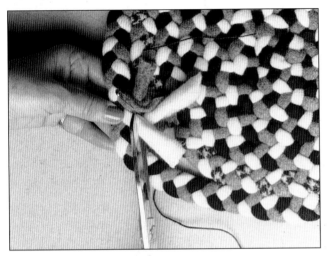

Cutting next loop even with edge

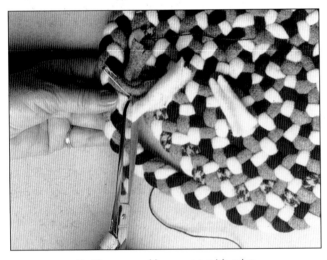

Cutting second loop even with edge

Figure 33

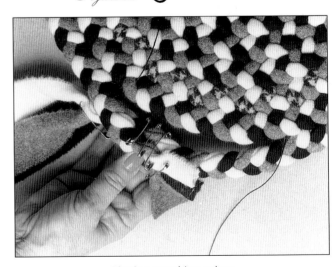

Pinning matching colors

20. Unbraid to the pinned loops. Take out any pins left on the ends. Cut the end of the braid so that only about 2 inches (5 cm) remains on the end of the braid.

Extra braid cut off

21. You will be starting to butt with only two strands in the final place (up), one on the left, and one on the right (figure 34). Hold firmly and remove the outside pin.

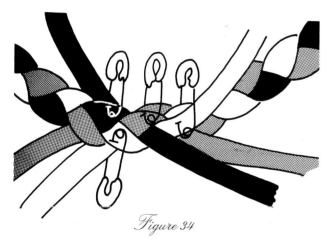

Figure 34

22. Insert the lacing needle into the front of the middle loop and pull the end up and out. Insert the needle into the front of the rear middle loop. Pull the loop up and out. Cross the front over the back, pull out any fullness, making sure the edges are turned in. Unpin and repin evenly with the side of the braid.

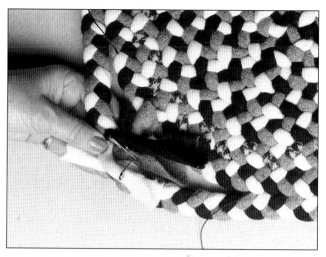

Third loop after first and second loops are pulled through and pinned

23. Work on the loop to the left. Insert the needle into the front loop, pull it out, cross over the back loop, pull out the fullness, and pin. Unpin and repin evenly with the side of the braid (figure 35).

Figure 35

24. Unpin the right loop. Pull the inside loop out of the braid, *slip your finger in where the loop came out, and insert the outside loop in the hole, pulling it toward the fold side.* Pull the fullness out, fold the edges in, cross over the back loop, and pin (figure 35). The last row is now woven together.

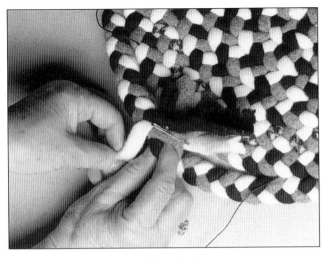

Putting fingers through braid where loop came out

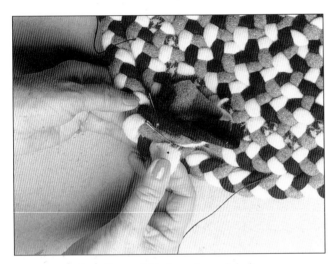

Inserting outside loop through hole

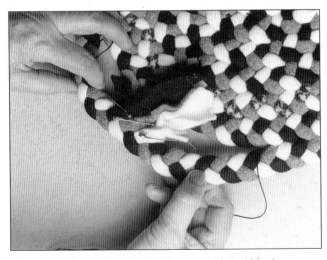

Crossing over and pinning even with inside edge

25. Unpin the loops to the right, cut evenly along the edge, and overcast firmly with matching thread.

26. Repeat with the middle and left side loops. All of the seams should fall between the rows so the joined ends don't show (figure 36).

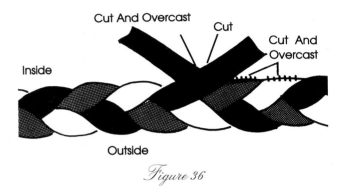

Figure 36

27. Lace the final 8 inches (20.5 cm) to the rug.

28. Weave the ends of the lacing thread through the loops until they meet, and tie.

Congratulations! You have just completed your oval braided rug. I'm sure you now have your own stories about this "first rug" to share with friends and family.

The Circle Braided Rug

▼ ▼ ▼

The circle is also an easy rug for the beginner. If your braid isn't even, you can accommodate the difference by spacing your skips closer or farther apart. If your braid widens, you can skip less often. If your braid narrows, you can skip more frequently. Of course, if you maintain a braid of consistent width, you will wind up with a smoother and more uniform rug.

A circle lends itself well to either a shaded rug or a hit-or-miss style. If you are shading, change one color at a time in various places all around the circle—not in one spot, as in the oval. If you are shading lighter, remove the darkest strand; if you are shading darker, remove the lightest strand.

Materials

Bluebell is a circle, 4 feet, 5 inches (1.2 m, 13 cm) wide. You will need about 11 pounds (5 kilos) of wool. It is a monochromatic rug in shades of blue and gray. Review the list of equipment you'll need on page 38. Make sure you have matching sewing thread.

Starting the Circle

1. *T-start* as in the oval directions, following steps 1-7 on pages 43–44.

2. Attach Braid-Aids, if you are using them.

Color Plan

Rows 1-5	Med. Blue Tweed	Med. Blue Tweed	Lt. Gray Tweed
Row 6	Darker Blue Tweed	Med. Blue Tweed	Blue/White Check
Rows 7 & 8	Med. Blue Tweed	Med. Blue Tweed	Blue/White Check
Row 9	Dark Blue	Med. Blue Tweed	Blue/White Check
Rows 10-12	Dark Blue	Dark Blue Tweed	Blue/White Check
Rows 13 & 14	Med. Blue	Dark Blue Tweed	Blue/White Check
Rows 15 & 16	Med. Blue	Dark Blue Tweed	Lt. Gray Tweed
Rows 17 & 18	Med. Blue	Lt. Gray Tweed	Lt. Gray Tweed
Rows 19-21	Wedgewood Blue	Lt. Gray Tweed	Lt. Gray Tweed
Row 22	Wedgewood Blue	Lt. Gray Tweed	Lt. Blue
Rows 23 & 24	Lt. Blue Tweed	Lt. Gray Tweed	Lt. Blue
Row 25	Lt. Blue Tweed	Med. Gray Tweed	Lt. Blue
Row 26	Blue & White Tweed	Med. Gray Tweed	Blue & White Tweed
Rows 27 & 28	Blue & White Tweed	Med. Gray Tweed	Med. Blue
Row 29	Blue & White Tweed	Med. Gray Tweed	Darker Blue
Row 30	Darker Blue & White Tweed	Med. Gray Tweed	Darker Blue
Row 31	Darker Blue & White Tweed	Darker Blue Tweed	Darker Blue
Rows 32-35	Dark Blue Tweed	Darker Blue Tweed	Darker Blue

3. Roll up one strand to 2 feet (61.5 cm) from the braid and pin to keep the strands from tangling.

4. Braid six twice overs as follows:

   a. Hold the *T* so the center tube has the fold on the left (figure 7, page 44).

   b. Pull the right tube over the center, keeping the fold on the left, and hold (figure 37a).

   c. Again, pull the tube on the right to the center, keeping the fold on the left (figure 37b).

   d. Pull the tube on the left to the center—pull tightly— and hold (leave the fold on the right). This one is called the pulled loop (figure 37c).

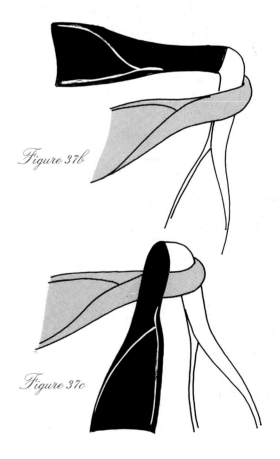

Figure 37b

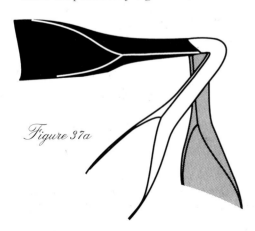

Figure 37a

Figure 37c

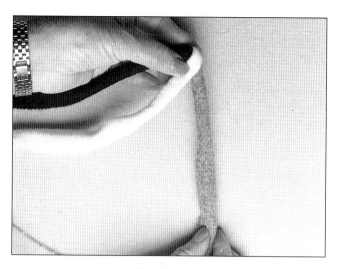

Pulling from right

Pulling from right again

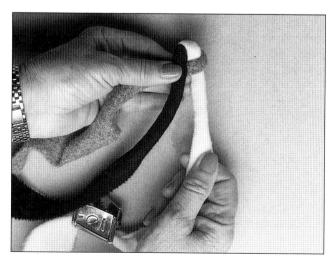

Pulling from left

5. Repeat steps a–c five more times (figures 38a, b, and c).

Figure 38a

Figure 38b

Figure 38c

6. On the third twice over, flat fold to the left the tube with the fold on the right, so that all the folds will be on the left. The center should have the curve braided in (figure 39).

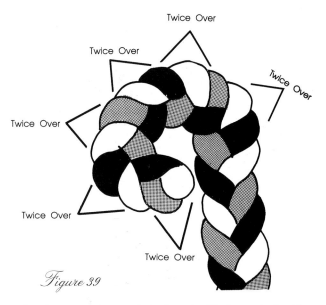

Twice Over
Twice Over
Twice Over
Twice Over
Twice Over
Twice Over

Figure 39

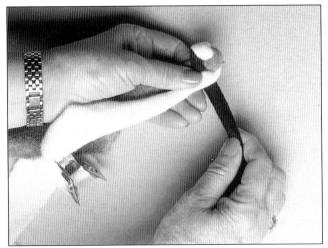

Pulling from right

7. After the six twice overs have been braided, put the braid into the clamp and braid normally for a the rest of the rug; that is, fold the edges in, pull from the right to the center and hold, then pull from the left to the center and hold, alternating from right to left (figures 8 and 9, page 45). When you stop, put a large safety pin through the loops. Figure 40 indicates all the key locations for making your circle.

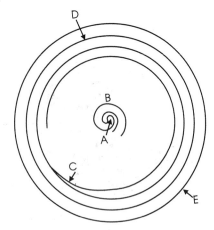

A - "T" Beginning
B - 6 Twice Overs
C - Rattail Area - 3rd To The Last Row
D - Butting Area - Next To The Last Row
E - Butting Area - Last Row

Figure 40

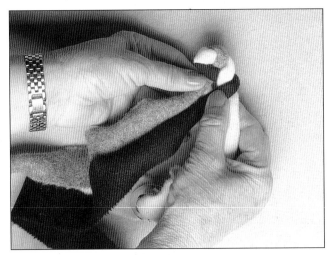

Pulling from right again

Lacing

1. Always lace on a flat surface. Take about 4 feet (1.2 m) of lacing thread, thread it into the tapestry needle, and knot.

Pulling from left

2. Make sure the right side of the rug is facing you, with the *T* positioned away from you, and to your left (figure 41a). Form the braid into a circle and hold together tightly. Insert the needle into the third pulled loop—through the wool—to attach the thread and hide it (figure 41a).

3. Insert the needle into the *T*, and take a 1/4-inch (1 cm) stitch half way between the bottom and the top (figure 41b). Pull. Lace the fourth loop, using the blunt end of the tapestry needle; pull (figure 41c).

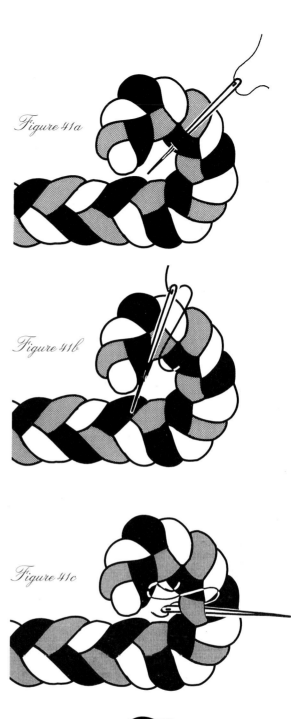

Figure 41a

Figure 41b

Figure 41c

Figure 41d

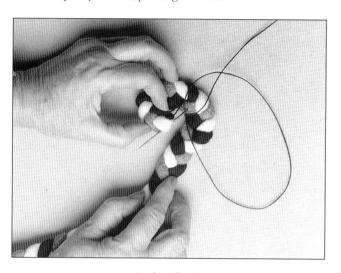

Lacing the T

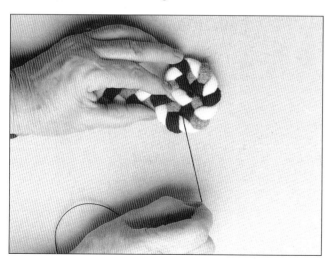

Pulling the stitch tightly at end of T

4. Take another 1/4-inch (1 cm) stitch into the end of the *T* (figure 41d), pull tightly, and switch to a lacing needle. The center of the circle should be closed tightly and the stitches hidden. The *T* is now laced.

Figure 41e

Figure 41f

5. Continue lacing—going between the loops. Lace from the braid you are attaching to the body of the rug (figures 41e and 41f).

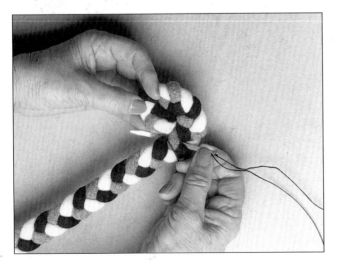

Lacing from the outside to the center

6. *Lace in every loop in the body of the rug. Skip only on the row you are attaching.* The skips will get farther apart as the circle gets bigger. For example, on row 1, lace one loop and skip one loop all the way around. On row 2, lace two and skip one—all the way around.

Tip Try to skip evenly around the rug; for example, if you are lacing five loops and skipping one, do it all the way around. Lace the row you are attaching, then lace the body of the rug; hold both braids flat, pull the lacing thread, and decide if you need to skip (figure 23, page 49).

7. Starting on row 4, put a T-pin in the skipped loop. Keep the pins in for four to five rows. Avoid skipping in the same place; alternate your skips (figure 22, page 49).

More Tips About Lacing and Skipping

▼ If the rug scallops, you are skipping too often. On the next row, try not to skip at all. This will take out the fullness. Then resume a normal pattern of skips.

▼ If the rug buckles in the center, you are not skipping enough. You need to take out your lacing until the rug is flat; then resume lacing, making sure to skip more often.

▼ A well-shaped circle is accomplished by skipping loops evenly and alternating your skips on the row you're attaching.

Changing Colors

Vary the place where you make your color changes. New colors should appear on the outside loop (figures 24 and 25, page 50 and page 51).

Rattailing

The method of rattailing is the same as for the oval rug directions except that you can rattail anywhere in your circle (see steps 3-7, figures 27 and 28, page 53. The larger the circle, the longer the rattail should be. For a chair pad, taper a 6-inch (15 cm) strip to an 8-inch (20.5 cm) strip. For larger circles, taper a 10-inch (25.5 cm) strip to a 20-inch (51 cm) strip.

Butting

Follow the oval rug directions for butting on page 54.

The Heart Braided Rug

▼ ▼ ▼

The heart is one of the most admired braided rugs. However, this shape is not for the beginner. It is best to make a few oval or circles first to learn to braid evenly, skip well, and practice doing twice overs. The heart requires practice; to ensure a well-balanced heart, you need to stop braiding at both the top and bottom v, and lace up to that point, so that you can braid the twice over in just the right spot.

Materials

"Country Heart" is 31 by 41 inches (79.5 x 105 cm) and requires about 4-1/2 pounds (2.1 kilos) of wool. Review the equipment list on page 38. Purchase matching sewing thread.

T-start

T-start as per the oval directions, steps 1-7, page 43 and page 43, then braid straight for 11 inches (28 cm) as per steps 1-7, page 45. Figure 42 diagrams all the key elements of the heart-shaped rug.

Twice overs

1. Braid one twice over.
   a. Take the tube on the left and braid (figure 43a).
   b. Take the tube from the *left* again and braid (figure 43b).
   c. Braid the tube from the *right* and pull tightly (figure 43c). The first center v is now braided in.

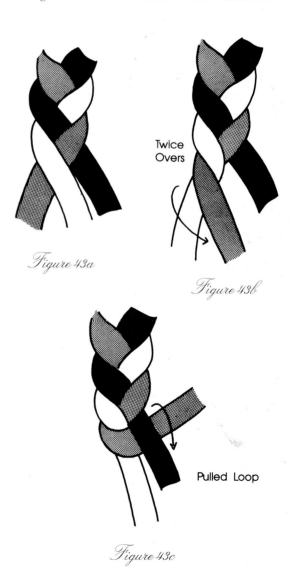

Twice Overs

Figure 43a

Figure 43b

Pulled Loop

Figure 43c

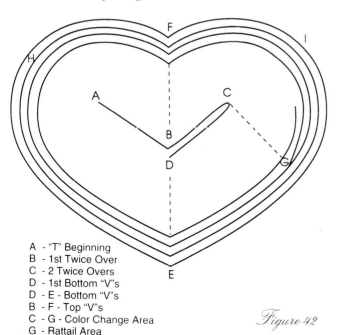

A - "T" Beginning
B - 1st Twice Over
C - 2 Twice Overs
D - 1st Bottom "V"s
D - E - Bottom "V"s
B - F - Top "V"s
C - G - Color Change Area
G - Rattail Area
H - 1st Butting Area
I - Last Butting Area

Figure 42

Color Plan

Rows 1-4	Dusty Rose	Mauve	Pink & Gray Check
Row 5	Plum	Mauve	Pink & Gray Check
Row 6	Plum	Maroon	Pink & Gray Check
Row 7	Plum	Maroon	Dark Blue Green
Row 8	Dark Blue	Maroon	Dark Blue Green
Row 9	Dark Blue	Medium Blue	Dark Blue Green
Row 10	Dark Turquoise	Medium Blue	Dark Blue Green
Row 11	Dark Turquoise	Medium Blue	Lt Blue & White Check
Row 12	Dusty Rose	Medium Blue	Lt Blue & White Check
Row 13	Dusty Rose	Light Pink	Pink & Gray Check
Row 14	Dusty Rose	Plum	Dark Pink & Gray Check
Row 15	Maroon	Plum	Dark Pink & Gray Check

2. Braid 11 inches (28 cm) more; then braid two twice overs, this time turning in the opposite direction.

   a. Take the tube on the right and braid (figure 44a).

   b. Take the next tube from the *right*, braid and hold (figure 44b).

   c. Braid the tube from the *left* and pull tightly (figure 44c).

   d. Repeat steps 2a, b, and c once more. This is the only time two twice overs are braided in (figure 11, page 46, and figure 42, page 67).

Figure 44a

Figure 44b

Figure 44c

Braiding

Braid another 11 inches (28 cm) and begin to lace.

Lacing

Lace the first 11 inches (28 cm) using either the reverse e method or the sewing method as shown in figures 12-18. Lace until the center *v* is reached.

Braiding and Lacing First V

1. Braid a single corner as in figures 44a, b, and c. Braid this corner so that the pulled loop on the row you are attaching falls *between* the twice over loops on row 1.

2. Lace as per figure 45.

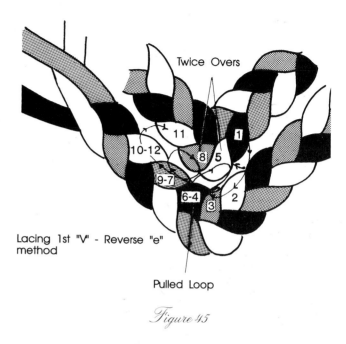

Lacing 1st "V" - Reverse "e" method

Figure 45

3. Continue lacing in reverse e method or sewing method until you reach the *T*.

4. Switch to a tapestry needle and sew the *T* as per the oval direction, steps 6-8, figure 19. Return the thread to your lacing needle and lace the rest of the heart in the regular way, going into every loop until the top *v* is reached.

Braiding and Lacing Top and Bottom Vs

1. Braid the top *v* as you did in figures 43a, b, and c, braiding twice from the left, then braiding a pulled loop from the right.

2. Braid the twice overs so that when lacing, you lace the twice overs, then skip the pulled loop on the body of the rug (figure 46).

3. Continue braiding and lacing until the curved end is reached. Lace this as you did the oval rug (page 49).

4. Continue braiding and lacing until you reach the bottom *v*.

5. Braid in a twice over as per figures 44a, b, and c. Braid the twice over so that the pulled loop on the braid you are attaching falls after the twice-over loops on the body of the rug.

6. Lace the twice-over loops, then skip the pulled loop.

7. Continue braiding, lacing, and braiding in *vs* until four rows are finished. Change one color as per color plan. Refer to figure 42 for color change area.

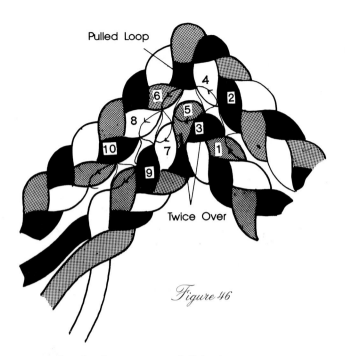

Pulled Loop

Twice Over

Figure 46

Continuing the Rug

Continue braiding, lacing, and changing colors as per the color chart until you have completed 13 rows.

Rattailing or Tapering

Rattailing is the same as in the oval; refer to figure 42 for the rattail area.

Butting

Rows 14 and 15 are the same as for the oval and circle; see figure 42 for the butting area.

General Rules for Lacing and Skipping

These rules are the same for the heart as for the oval and circle, with one exception: try to force skips farther around the curve toward both the top and bottom vs. This fills out the heart shape.

Tip Don't skip so much that the rug scallops (figure 47).

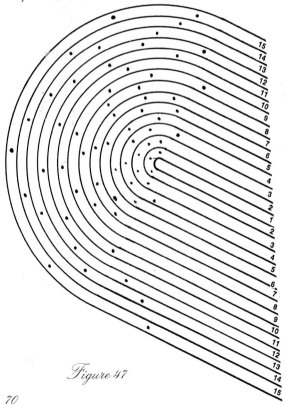

Figure 47

The Strip Braided Rug

▼ ▼ ▼

*S*imply braiding straight rows with the traditional three-strand braid creates the strip rug. Each of the rows must be the same width, and your lacing even, or your rug will pull out of shape.

Materials

"Forest Green Strip" is a rectangle 26 x 49 inches (66 x 124.5 cm). You will need about 6 pounds (2.7 kg) of wool. Review the list of equipment you'll need on page 38. Make sure you have matching sewing thread as well as clear nylon thread for stitching across the ends.

Starting the row

1. Start each row by folding the edges in, then folding together again, as in a regular braid, and pin to hold (figure 29, page 54).

2. Put the three strands into a clamp. The pins will hold the braid in place. (See photo under figure 29.) Put a fourth pin across the braid to keep it from unbraiding.

3. Braid to the length you want your finished rug to be.

4. Lace the center two rows together.

Forest Green Strip Rug
Color Plan
26" x 49" (66 x 124.5 cm)

Color Plan

Row 1	Dark Green	Light Green	Red/Green Plaid
Row 2	Dark Green	Dark Green	Dark Green
Rows 3	Dark Green	Dark Green	Light Green
Row 4-6	Dark Green	Medium Green	Light Green
Row 7	Dark Green	Dark Green	Light Green
Row 8	Dark Green	Dark Green	Dark Green
Rows 9-11	Dark Green	Medium Green	Light Green
Row 12	Dark Green	Dark Green	Dark Green
Rows 13-15	Dark Green	Light Green	Red/Green Plaid
Rows 16-18	Dark Green	Dark Green	Dark Green

18 17 16 15 14 13 12 11 10 9 8 7 6 5 4 3 2 1 1 2 3 4 5 6 7 8 9 10 11 12 13 14 15 16 17 18

Lining up the rug on the cutting mat

5. As you braid more rows, add them on one side of the center, then on the other side of the center.

6. It is important to lace in every loop. Never skip on a strip rug.

7. I lace on a rotary cutting mat. This way I can make sure that the sides of the rug are straight.

8. Leave at least 4 inches of lacing thread on both ends of each row.

9. After adding your desired number of rows, it's time to finish off the ends.

10. Use the lines on the cutting mat to determine where the ends need to be sewn.

Mark both ends with masking tape. Note: I then took my rug to a woman who has an industrial sewing machine, and she sewed the ends. I recommend using a clear, 100% nylon thread so the stitching is as invisible as possible.

11. Cut the excess braid evenly along the edge, leaving some for the fringe.

12. Put the lacing thread into your lacing needle, and lace back into the body of your rug for a few loops, and cut it off. This, plus the machine sewing, should make a sturdy end.

13. Another method of finishing a strip rug is to machine stitch, as in step 10, then cut the excess close to the stitching, and sew on a binding.

Creating a Pattern

A strip rug is a great rug to work in a pattern. Here's one possibility:

Row 2   3 strands of dark green

Row 3   2 strands of dark green and 1 light green

Row 4   1 strand of dark green, 1 light green, and 1 medium green.

By lacing the dark green on row four between the two dark greens on row three, you create a pattern (figure 48).

Finished rug detail

Figure 48

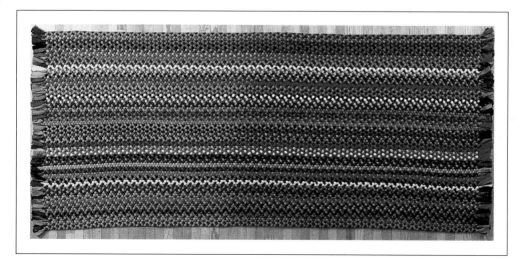

Blue, purple, and fuschia runner, 31" x 75" (79.5 x 190 cm), designed by Marie Griswold, braided by Carrie Freyermuth

The Five-Strand Rug

▼ ▼ ▼

The five-strand or multi-strand rug is considered an advanced rug to make because of the need to handle so many strands during the braiding process. Once the braid has been made, the multi-strand rug is laced as usual. The multi-strand is challenging but adds considerable interest to the standard three-strand rug. It may also account for the attraction it holds for some of the new folks just discovering braiding. It is a stunning rug whether made into an oval or a circle.

Materials

"Colonial Colors" is a three- and five-strand braided rug. Plan on approximately 3-1/2 pounds (1.6 kg) of wool to make it. There are several ways you can handle braiding with five strands.

Method #1

Using heavy weight wool, cut all of your strips 1 inch wide. A wool cutter comes in handy with this method. Iron the strips in half.

Photo © Glen Janssen

Colonial Colors Three and Five-Strand
25 1/2" x 39" (64.8 x 99 cm)

Color Plan

Rows 1-5	Maroon	Off-White	Navy	Gray Tweed	Dk. Gray
Rows 6-7	Maroon	Camel	Navy	Gray Tweed	Dk. Gray
Row 8	Maroon	Camel	Dk. Gray		
Row 9	Maroon	Maroon	Maroon		
Rows 10	Navy	Navy	Navy		

Cutting the strips

Method #2

Cut or rip strips 1-1/2 inches wide, using medium weight wool. Fold edges in as per your regular braid, and baste the strips. This is a time-consuming process, but it makes a smooth, even braid (figure 49).

Method #3

Cut or rip strips as in Method 2, and then put Braid Aids on all five strips. Method 3 is cumbersome to work with but helps if you iron in your folds.

My "Colonial Colors Rug" was made using Method 2. I used Method 1 to create the "Merry-Go-Round Rug" (See Color Plan, page 96).

1. Have five strips ready, and start by combining two strips. Baste edges as shown in figure 50. Take strips 3, 4, and 5, turn edges in, and attach the three strips to the center, with the folded edge on the left side (figure 51).

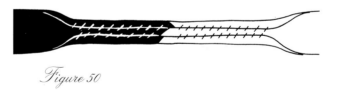

Figure 50

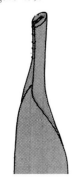

Figure 49

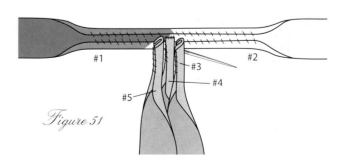

#1   #2   #3   #4   #5

Figure 51

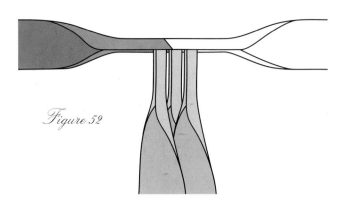

Figure 52

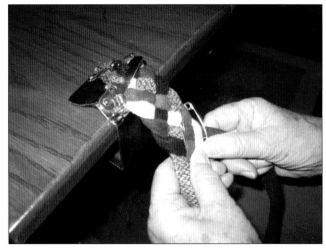

Braiding clamp holding first 4 inches of braid

2. Fold the top half of the combined strips over the bottom half, and blind stitch 2 to 3 inches (5 to 7.5 cm) on both sides of the center seam, enclosing the tube (figure 52).

3. You have now completed the *T*. Finish by folding beginning strips 1 and 2 over strip 3, 4, and 5. Start braiding by pulling strip 2 over strip 3 and under strip 4. Then pull strip 1 over strip 5 and under strip 2. Continue by pulling from the right, over and under, and then from the left, go over and under, keeping the folds to the left (figure 53).

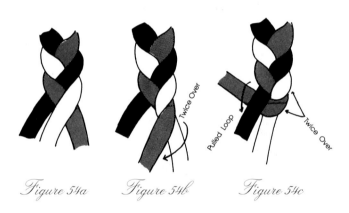

Figure 54a   *Figure 54b*   *Figure 54c*

4. Continue braiding until the center is 13 inches long. Then do five twice-overs (figures 54a, 54b, 54c). This method turns your corner. Continue braiding for approximately 36 inches. Lacing a five-strand rug is the same as lacing a three-strand, as shown below.

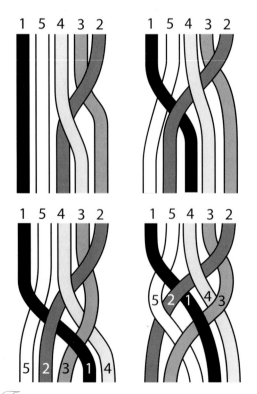

Figure 53

Figure 55

Figure 56

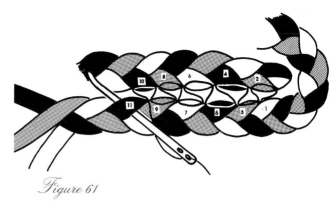

Figure 61

Figure 57

5. Lace the center row (figures 55–60). After lacing around the *T*, begin regular lacing (figure 61). Note: Multi-strand braids do not lie flat when lacing corners. One method to help ease the row you are attaching is to run lacing thread through the inside of the braid. Pull on the lacing thread, and it will gather the braid and thus help it to contour to the rug.

6. Continue braiding, and lace for seven rows. Bind off two strands in as invisible manner as possible.

7. End your continuous braid by rattailing row 8, and butting rows 9 and 10.

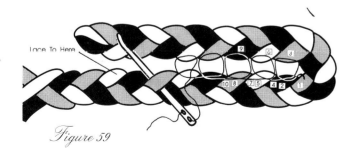

Figure 58

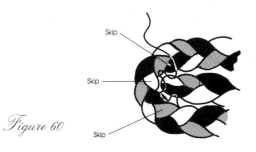

Figure 59

Lace To Here

Figure 60

Skip

Skip

Skip

Color Plans for 20 Rugs

▼   ▼   ▼

Bittersweet
2'3" x 3'3" (69 x 100 cm)

Color Plan

Rows 1-5	Orange	Camel	Dk. Brown Tweed
Row 6	Orange Plaid	Camel	Dk. Brown Tweed
Rows 7-9	Orange Plaid	Camel	Lt. Tan
Row 10	Orange Plaid	Camel	Med. Rust
Row 11	Orange Plaid	Taupe	Med. Rust
Row 12	Orange	Taupe	Med. Rust
Row 13	Orange	Taupe	Dk. Brown Tweed
Row 14	Orange	Dk. Brown Tweed	Dk. Brown Tweed
Rows 15-17	Dk. Rust	Dk. Brown Tweed	Dk. Brown Tweed

Amish
45" x 57" (115.5 x 146.5 cm)

Color Plan

Rows 1-5	Taupe	Mauve	Mauve & Black Plaid
Rows 6 & 7	Dusty Rose	Mauve	Mauve & Black Plaid
Rows 8 & 9	Lt. Dusty Rose	Mauve	Magenta (rattail)
Row 10	Lt. Dusty Rose	Black	Magenta
Row 11	Black	Black	Magenta
Row 12	Black	Royal Blue	Magenta
Rows 13 & 14	Wedgewood Blue	Royal Blue	Magenta
Row 15	Wedgewood Blue	Royal Blue	Wedgewood Blue
Row 16	Wedgewood Blue	Dk. Turquoise	Wedgewood Blue
Row 17	Wedgewood Blue	Dk. Turquoise	Med. Turquoise
Rows 18 & 19	Silver Gray	Dk. Turquoise	Med. Turquoise
Row 20	Silver Gray	Silver Gray	Med. Turquoise
Row 21	Silver Gray	Dusty Rose	Dk. Turquoise
Row 22	Magenta	Dusty Rose	Dk. Turquoise
Row 23	Magenta	Lt. Dusty Rose	Mauve
Row 24	Magenta	Med. Mauve	Mauve
Row 25	Magenta	Black	Mauve
Row 26	Magenta	Black	Mauve & Black Plaid
Row 27	Black	Black	Maroon
Row 28	Black	Black	Black

Americana
30" x 42" (77 x 108 cm)

Color Plan

Rows 1-7	Red	Gray	Blue/Red Plaid (rattail)
Row 8	Red	Red	Blue/Red Plaid
Row 9	Red	Red	Red
Row 10	Red	Navy	Blue/Red Plaid
Row 11	Navy	Navy	Blue/Red Plaid
Row 12	Navy	Navy	Navy
Rows 13-15	Navy	Gray	Blue/Red Plaid
Row 16	Navy	Red	Blue/Red Plaid
Row 17	Navy	Red	Red
Row 18	Red	Red	Red
Row 19	Navy	Navy	Navy

Country Spring Heart
30" x 40" (77 x 103 cm)

Color Plan

Rows 1-3	White	Med. Blue	Lt. Blue
Row 4	Lt. Pink	Med. Blue	Lt. Blue
Row 5	Lt. Pink	Med. Blue	Blue Gray Tweed
Row 6	Dusty Rose	Med. Blue	Blue Gray Tweed
Row 7	Dusty Rose	Med. Purple	Blue Gray Tweed
Row 8	Dusty Rose	Med. Purple	White
Row 9	Lt. Pink	Med. Purple	White
Row 10	Lt. Pink	Lt. Yellow	White
Row 11	Lt. Pink	Lt. Blue	White
Row 12	Med. Blue	Lt. Blue	White
Row 13	Med. Blue	Lt. Blue	Med. Green
Row 14	Med. Blue	Dusty Rose	Dusty Rose
Row 15	Dusty Rose	Dusty Rose	Dusty Rose

Western
3' x 5' (92.5 x 152.4 cm)

Color Plan

Rows 1-5	Lt. Tan	Lt. Rust	Lt. Tan Herringbone
Rows 6	Lt. Tan	Lt. Rust	Camel
Rows 7 & 8	Brown/Rust Plaid	Lt. Rust	Camel
Row 9	Brown/Rust Plaid	Taupe	Camel
Row 10	Brown/Rust Plaid	Taupe	Taupe
Row 11	Black	Taupe	Taupe
Row 12	Brown Herringbone	Taupe	Taupe
Row 13	Brown Herringbone	Taupe	Camel
Row 14	Brown Herringbone	Beige	Camel
Rows 15-17	Rust Herringbone	Beige	Camel
Row 18	Rust Herringbone	Rust Herringbone	Camel
Row 19	Rust Herringbone	Brown/Beige Check	Camel
Row 20	Rust	Brown/Beige Check	Camel
Row 21	Rust	Brown/Beige Check	Dk. Brown
Row 22	Rust	Dk. Brown	Dk. Brown
Row 23	Black	Dk. Brown	Dk. Brown

Kaleidoscope
45" x 45" (115.5 x 115.5 cm)

Color Plan

Rows 1-8	Med. Blue	Magenta	Blue Speckled
Rows 9-11	Med. Blue	Dark Purple	Blue Speckled
Rows 12 & 13	Med. Turquoise	Dark Purple	Blue Speckled
Row 14	Med. Turquoise	Lt. Turquoise	Blue Speckled
Rows 15 & 16	Med. Turquoise	Lt. Turquoise	Blue Gray Tweed
Rows 17 & 18	Med. Turquoise	Wedgewood Blue	Blue Gray Tweed
Rows 19-21	Bright Blue	Wedgewood Blue	Blue Gray Tweed
Row 22	Magenta	Wedgewood Blue	Blue Gray Tweed
Rows 23 & 24	Magenta	Wedgewood Blue	Blue Speckled
Rows 25-27	Magenta	Dk. Blue & Black Plaid	Purple
Rows 28-30	Royal Blue	Dk. Blue & Black Plaid	Purple

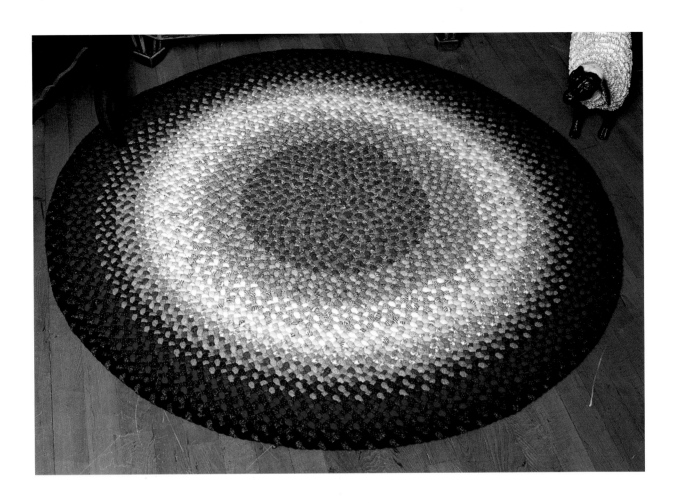

Coals On The Hearth
4' circle (123 cm)

Color Plan

Rows 1-10	Med. Gray/Red Plaid	Med. Gray	B&W Check
Rows 11-13	Light Gray	Med. Gray	B&W Check
Row 14	Light Gray	Med. Gray	Lighter B&W Check
Rows 15 & 16	Light Gray	White	Lighter B&W Check
Rows 17-19	Light Gray	White	Silver Gray
Row 20	Light Gray	Gray & White Check	Silver Gray
Row 21	Med. Gray	Gray & White Check	Med. Gray
Rows 22 & 23	Med. Gray	Med. Gray/Red Plaid	Dk. Gray
Rows 24-25	Med. Gray	B&R Check	Dk. Gray
Row 26	Old Red	B&R Check	Dk. Gray
Rows 27 & 28	Old Red	B&R Check	Black Plaid
Row 29	Black	B&R Check	Black Plaid
Row 30	Black	Black	Black Plaid

Victorian
4'9" scalloped (146 cm)

Color Plan

Rows 1-10	Lt. Beige Tweed	Lt. Taupe	Med. Taupe
Rows 11-13	Lt. Beige Tweed	Med. Taupe	Med. Taupe
Rows 14-16	Med. Taupe Tweed	Med. Taupe	Med. Taupe
Row 17	Med. Taupe Tweed	Med. Taupe	Black
Row 18	Blue Tweed	Med. Taupe	Black
Rows 19-20	Blue Tweed	Blue Plaid	Black
On Row 20, make six 6-inch braids an equal distance apart			
Row 21	Blue Plaid	Blue Plaid	Black
Row 22	Blue Plaid	Blue Plaid	Taupe
Row 23	Blue Plaid	Dusty Rose Tweed	Taupe
Row 24	Dusty Rose	Dusty Rose Tweed	Taupe
Row 25	Dusty Rose	Dusty Rose Tweed	Lt. Taupe Tweed
Row 26	Dusty Rose	Lt. Taupe	Lt. Taupe Tweed
Rows 27 & 28	Pink	Lt. Taupe	Lt. Taupe Tweed
Row 29	Pink	Lt. Taupe Tweed	Lt. Taupe Tweed
Row 30	Lt. Taupe Tweed	Lt. Taupe Tweed	Lt. Taupe Tweed

Nursery
5' x 7' (1.5 x 2.2 m)

Color Plan

Rows 1-5	Lt. Blue	Lt. Blue & White Plaid	Silver Gray
Row 6	Lt. Blue	Lt. Blue & White Plaid	Med. Gray
Row 7	Med. Blue	Lt. Blue & White Plaid	Med. Gray
Row 8	Med. Blue	Lt. Blue & White Plaid	Taupe
Row 9	Med. Blue	Med. Blue & White Plaid	Taupe
Rows 10 & 11	Dusty Rose	Med. Blue & White Plaid	Taupe
Row 12	Dusty Rose	Med. Taupe	Taupe
Row 13	Golden Brown	Med. Taupe	Taupe
Row 14	Golden Brown	Med. Taupe	Lt. Gray
Row 15	Golden Brown	Med. Gray	Lt. Gray
Row 16	Silver Gray	Med. Gray	Lt. Gray
Row 17	Lt. Green Plaid	Med. Gray	Lt. Gray
Row 18	Lt. Green Plaid	Med. Gray	Lt. Green
Row 19	Lt. Green Plaid	Lt. Yellow	Lt. Green
Rows 20 & 21	Lt. Yellow Green	Lt. Yellow	Lt. Green
Row 22	Lt. Yellow Green	Green & Yellow Plaid	Lt. Green
Row 23	Med. Green	Green & Yellow Plaid	Lt. Green
Row 24	Med. Green	Blue/Green Plaid	Lt. Green
Row 25	Med. Green	Blue/Green Plaid	Dk. Blue/Green Plaid
Row 26	Med. Green	Med. Blue Plaid	Dk. Blue/Green Plaid
Rows 27 & 28	Med. Blue	Med. Blue Plaid	Dk. Blue/Green Plaid
Row 29	Med. Blue	Med. Blue Plaid	Dk. Blue
Row 30	Med. Blue	Med. Blue Plaid	Taupe
Row 31	Med. Blue	Navy & White Tweed	Taupe
Row 32	Lt. Blue	Navy & White Tweed	Taupe
Row 33	Lt. Blue	Navy & White Tweed	Silver Gray
Row 34	Lt. Blue	Navy & White Tweed	Med. Blue Plaid
Row 35	Med. Blue	Navy & White Tweed	Med. Blue Plaid
Row 36	Dk. Blue	Dk. Blue	Navy Plaid

Bits and Pieces
60" circle (152 cm)

A hit-or-miss rug using scraps of brown, taupe, camel, beige, and plaids.

Nantucket
34" x 58" (87 x 149 cm)

Color Plan

Rows 1-5	Med. Blue	Gray	Blue Green Check
Rows 6-7	Med. Blue	Gray	Blue/White Check
Row 8	Med. Blue	Gray	Lt. Gray
Row 9	Lt. Green	Gray	Lt. Gray
Row 10	Lt. Green	Lt. Green	Lt. Gray
Row 11	Lt. Green	Lt. Green	Gray Check
Row 12	Lt. Green	Blue Green	Gray Check
Rows 13 & 14	Med. Green	Blue Green	Gray Check
Row 15	Med. Green	Blue Green	Med. Blue
Rows 16 & 17	Olive Green	Blue Green	Med. Blue
Rows 18 & 19	Olive Green	Blue Green	Blue Green
Row 20	Olive Green	Blue Green	Darker Green
Row 21	Olive Green	Darker Green	Darker Green

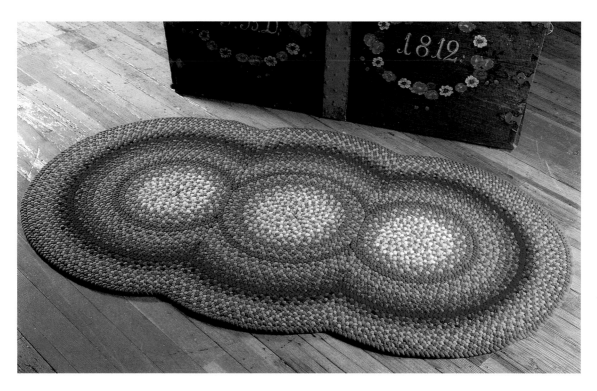

Heather Roses
3'4" x 5'8" (103 x 173 cm)

Color Plan

Rows 1-6	Lt. Olive Green	Lt. Pink	Olive Tweed
Rows 7 & 8	Lt. Olive Green	Brick Red	Olive Tweed
Row 9	Med. Olive Green	Brick Red	Olive Tweed
Rows 10 & 11 (on center circle only)	Med. Olive Green	Taupe	Olive Tweed
Row 12 (rattailed into vs where circles join)	Med. Olive Green	Med. Olive Green	Med. Olive Green
Remaining rows are butted			
Row 13	Med. Olive Green	Taupe	Dusty Rose
Rows 14 & 15	Brick Red	Taupe	Dusty Rose
Row 16	Brick Red	Taupe	Maroon Tweed
Row 17	Brick Red	Gray/Maroon Tweed	Maroon Tweed
Row 18	Old Red	Gray/Maroon Tweed	Maroon Tweed
Row 19	Old Red	Old Red	Old Red
Row 20	Old Red	Brick Red	Dk. Tweed
Row 21	Taupe	Brick Red	Dk. Tweed
Row 22	Taupe	Brick Red	Pink/Gray Tweed
Row 23	Lt. Olive Green	Brick Red	Pink/Gray Tweed
Row 24	Lt. Olive Green	Med. Olive Green	Pink/Gray Tweed
Row 25	Lt. Olive Green	Med. Olive Green	Med. Olive Green
Row 26	Med. Olive Green	Med. Olive Green	Med. Olive Green

My Valentine
30" x 40" (77 x 103 cm)

Color Plan

Rows 1-5	Dusty Rose	Med. Mauve	Multi-Colored Stripe
Row 6	Dusty Rose	Lt. Mauve	Multi-Colored Stripe
Rows 7 & 8	Dusty Rose	Lt. Pink	Multi-Colored Stripe
Rows 9 & 10	Pink	Lt. Pink	Multi-Colored Stripe
Row 11	Pink	Lt. Mauve	Multi-Colored Stripe
Row 12	Dusty Rose	Lt. Mauve	Maroon Plaid
Row 13	Dusty Rose	Dk. Mauve	Maroon Plaid
Row 14	Dk. Mauve	Dk. Mauve	Maroon Plaid

Favorite Colors
36" x 47" (92.5 x 120.5 cm)

Color Plan

Rows 1-3	Silver Gray	Lt. Blue	Lt. Blue
Row 4	Silver Gray	Lt. Blue	Dusty Rose
Row 5	Med. Gray	Lt. Blue	Dusty Rose
Row 6	Med. Gray	Med. Blue	Dusty Rose
Row 7	Med. Gray	Med. Blue	Med. Blue
Row 8	Med. Gray	Med. Blue	Dusty Rose
Rows 9 & 10	Med. Gray	Lt. Blue	Dusty Rose
Row 11	Lt. Blue	Lt. Blue	Dusty Rose
Row 12	Lt. Blue	Lt. Blue	Med. Blue
Row 13	Lt. Blue	Med. Blue	Med. Blue
Row 14	Navy Blue	Med. Blue	Med. Blue
Row 15	Navy Blue	Navy Blue	Navy Blue

Watermelon
18" x 25" (46 x 64 cm)

Color Plan

Rows 1-5	Solid Red
Rows 6-8	Red with Black Seeds
Row 9	Solid Red (rattail)
Row 10	1 Red, 2 Greenish White (butted)
Row 11	Solid Greenish White (butted)
Row 12	Solid Dk. Green (butted)

Santa Fe Strip
22" x 40" rectangle (56.5 x 102.5 cm)

Color Plan

Row 1	Turquoise	Turquoise	Gray Plaid
Row 2	Turquoise	Silver Gray	Gray Plaid
Row 3	Turquoise	Silver Gray	Silver Gray
Row 4	Turquoise	Turquoise	Silver Gray
Row 5	Turquoise	Turquoise	Turquoise
Row 6	Turquoise	Turquoise	Rust
Row 7	Turquoise	Camel	Rust
Row 8	Camel	Camel	Rust
Row 9	Camel	Camel	Camel
Row 10	Camel	Camel	Rust
Row 11	Camel	Turquoise	Gray Plaid
Rows 12 & 13	Turquoise	Turquoise	Gray Plaid
Row 14	Turquoise	Turquoise	Turquoise

Photo © Glen Janssen

The Marly Rose
54" x 70" (136.2 x 177.8 cm)

Color Plan

Rows 1-4	Pink	Dusty Rose	Lt. Lavender
Row 5	Pink	Dusty Rose	Plum
Rows 6-8	Lavender Tweed	Dusty Rose	Plum
Row 9	Lavender Tweed	Burgundy	Plum
Row 10	Burgundy	Burgundy	Plum

Joining Row

Row 11	Burgundy	Burgundy	Burgundy
Row 12	Burgundy	Burgundy	Dk. Burgundy Tweed
Row 13	Burgundy	Dk. Mauve	Dk. Burgundy Tweed
Row 14	Lt. Burgundy Tweed	Dk. Mauve	Dk. Burgundy Tweed
Rows 15-17	Lt. Burgundy Tweed	Dk. Mauve	Dusty Rose
Row 18	Lavender	Dusty Rose	Dusty Rose
Row 19	Lavender	Dusty Rose	Pink
Row 20-21	Lavender	Lt. Lavender Tweed	Pink
Row 22	Lavender	Lt. Lavender Tweed	Darker Pink
Rows 23-24	Lavender	Mauve Tweed	Darker Pink
Row 25	Lavender	Mauve Tweed	Lilac
Row 26	Burgundy	Mauve Tweed	Lilac
Row 27	Burgundy	Mauve Tweed	Lilac
Row 28	Burgundy	Burgundy	Burgundy

Photo © Glen Janssen

Graduation Bouquet
30 ¹/₂" x 42" (77.5 x 106.7 cm)

Color Plan

Rows 1-7	Kelly Green	Dk. Purple	Purple & Green Plaid
Rows 8,9,10	Med. Purple	Dk. Purple	Purple & Green Plaid
Row 11	Med. Purple	Dk. Purple	Purple & Green Plaid
Rows 12 & 13	Med. Purple	Multi-Color Tweed	Dk. Mauve
Rows 14 & 15	Lt. Blue	Multi-Color Tweed	Dk. Mauve
Row 16	Lt. Blue	Med. Blue Plaid	Dk. Mauve
Row 17	Dk. Multi-Color Plaid	Med. Blue Plaid	Dk. Mauve
Row 18	Dk. Purple	Med. Blue Plaid	Dk. Mauve
Row 19	Dk. Purple	Dk. Blue Plaid	Dk. Mauve
Row 20	Dk. Purple	Dk. Blue Plaid	Darker Purple

Photo © Glen Janssen

Merry-Go-Round
Three, Five and Seven-Strand Rug
32" x 48" (81.3 x 121.9 cm)

Color Plan

Rows 1-3	Navy	Dk. Gray	Dk. Gray Tweed	Off-White	Maroon		
Rows 4-5	Navy	Dk. Gray	Lt. Gray Tweed	Off-White	Maroon		
Row 6 & 7	Camel	Dk. Gray	Lt. Gray Tweed	Off-White	Maroon		
Row 8	Camel	Dk. Gray	Maroon				
Row 9	Maroon	Maroon	Maroon				
Row 10	Navy	Navy	Navy				
Row 11	Navy	Navy	Maroon	Off-White	Beige	Taupe	Maroon Tweed
Row 12	Navy	Navy	Navy				

Photo © Michael Drejza

Megan's Bright
29" x 41" (73.7 x 104.1 cm)

Color Plan

Rows 1-3	Magenta	Multicolored Tweed	Royal Blue
Row 4	Magenta	Multicolored Tweed	Baby Blue
Rows 5-6	Gold	Multicolored Tweed	Baby Blue
Row 7	Gold	Flat Side Of Bright Plaid	Baby Blue
Row 8	Gold	Flat Side Of Bright Plaid	Medium Blue
Rows 9-10	Dark Purple	Flat Side Of Bright Plaid	Medium Blue
Row 11	Dark Purple	Flat Side Of Bright Plaid	Medium Dark Purple
Row 12-16	Magenta	Flat Side Of Bright Plaid	Medium Dark Purple
Row 17-18	Dark Blue	Flat Side Of Bright Plaid	Medium Dark Purple
Row 19	Dark Blue	Flat Side Of Bright Plaid	Dark Purple

Gallery of Contemporary Rug Braiders

▼ ▼ ▼

Designer: **Lucy Long Armour**

Photos © Suzanne Ensor Ryan and Barry Ryan

Lucy Long Armour signed up for Nancy Young's rug braiding class as a neophyte rug hooker, interested in learning to braid borders for her rugs. She immediately became hooked on braiding, appreciating not only the beauty of braided rugs but their practicality as well. As a woman presiding over a household bustling with boys and large dogs, she serenely braids on, surrounded by male and canine chaos. Her rugs show a talent for creativity and unique design.

Top: Shanghai, 78 x 52" (198 x 132 cm)

Bottom: Wooly Worm, 74 x 28" (188 x 71 cm)

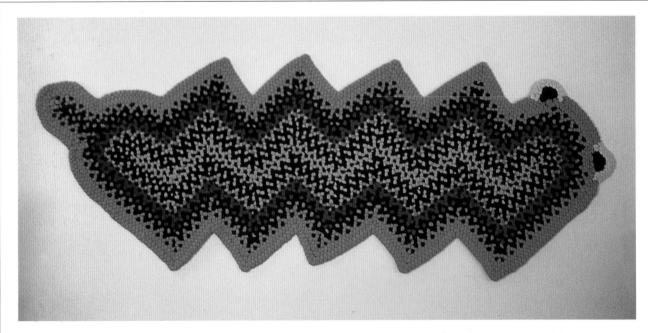

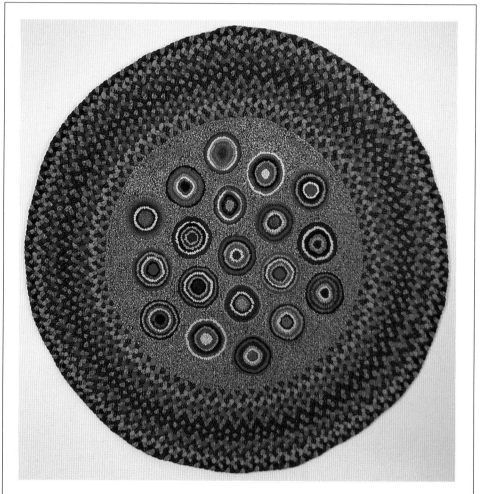

Top: Circus, 40" (101.6 cm) round

Bottom: Cirque, 36" (91 cm) round

Designer: **Verna Cox**

A resident of Verona Island, Maine, Verna Cox has written a number of braiding manuals, has produced several instructional videotapes, and designs color plans for braiders.

She is dedicated to teaching quality rug braiding and is well qualified to do so. A highly skilled and experienced braider, Verna once had a rug displayed in the Smithsonian, and has another hanging in the Maine room of the National 4-H Headquarters in Washington, D.C.

Right:
Quartet of Hearts, 45" (114.3 cm) round

Bottom:
Confetti, 2 x 3' (61.5 cm x 92.5 cm)

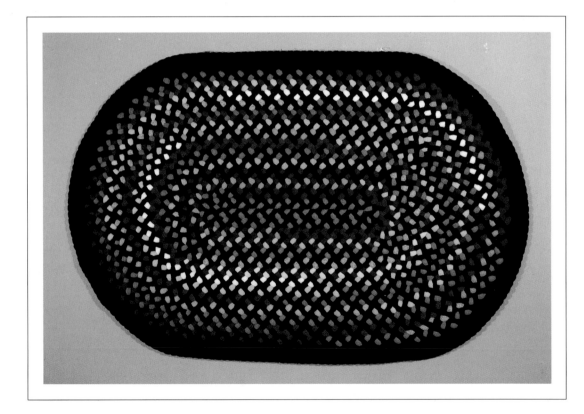

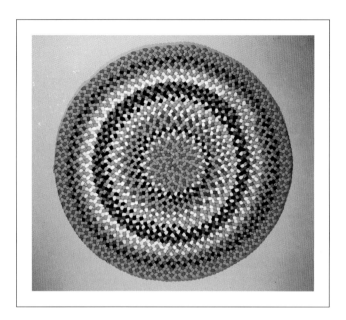

Top:
Sea Breeze, 30" (77cm) round

Bottom:
Winter Cheer, 2 x 3' (61.5 x 92.5 cm)

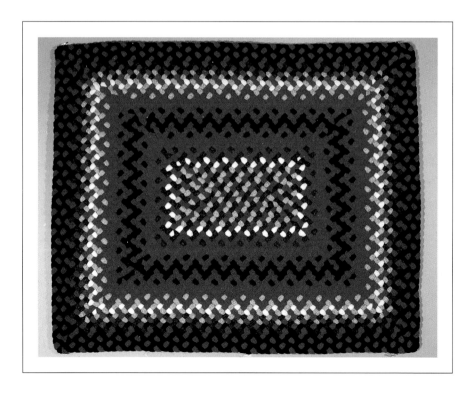

Designer: **Anne Eastwood**
Photos © Richard Church

Anne Eastwood's grandmother taught her to braid rugs many years ago. The rugs were actually plaited and sewn together with heavy thread. In 1960, Anne took her first formal lessons from Helen Howard Feeley, the author of *The Complete Book of Rug Braiding.*

Soon Anne began braiding rugs on consignment. Her first dining room rug commission earned her enough money to buy 12 acres of land in the Massachusetts Berkshires where she and her husband had a home built. She taught rug braiding for six years and then moved to Connecticut, where she continued to braid and teach. She managed to keep up these activities even during the busy years of raising five children.

She and her husband retired in 1990 and moved to Lake Placid, Florida, where Anne teaches, holds camps, and works on commissions. She is internationally known for her rug hooking and braiding. After braiding so many round, oval, square, and rectangular rugs, she finds it both exciting and challenging to create new shapes, such as the ones shown here.

Top:
Butterfly, 16 $^{1}/_{2}$ x 18 $^{1}/_{2}$" (41.9 x 47 cm)

Bottom left:
Anne Eastwood holding *Humble Beginnings,* 16 $^{1}/_{2}$" (41.9 cm) round, a hooked and braided chairpad designed by Jane McGoan Flynn for Primco Patterns, a division of House of Price, Inc.

Bottom right:
Bluefish, 18 x 28" (45.7 x 71.1 cm)

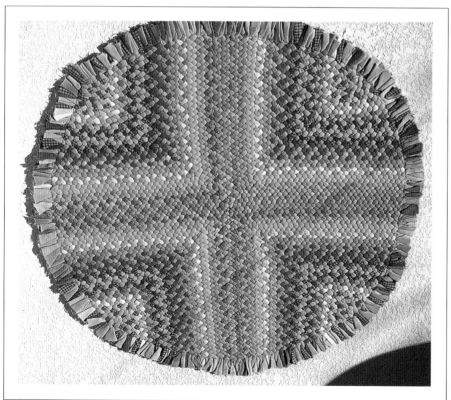

Top right:
Christmas Pleasure, 18 x 22" (45.7 x 55.9 cm)

Top left:
One Ripe Apple, 22 x 24" (55.9 x 61 cm)

Bottom left:
The Cross, 37" (94 cm) round

103

Designers: **Barbara Fisher** and **Janet Fitzgerald**

Barbara Fisher has been braiding rugs and teaching for 50 years. What began as a necessity to provide a warm rug for her family has become her passion. She developed her own technique for butting rows together, known as the "The Perfect Butt," which she has trademarked. She also invented and trademarked "The Counted Loop" method whereby, by counting loops, you can actually braid an entire rug before beginning to lace. She continues to share her lifelong love of braiding rugs by teaching, lecturing, and conducting workshops.

Janet Fitzgerald is Barbara's oldest daughter, and she also teaches, demonstrates, and assists with workshops. In addition, she manages the business side of their business, the Braided Rug Shop, as Barbara would be the first to admit that she would rather be braiding than managing the shop!

Top:
Long-Sided Octagon

Bottom left:
Janet (left) and Barbara (right)

Bottom right:
More Hexagons

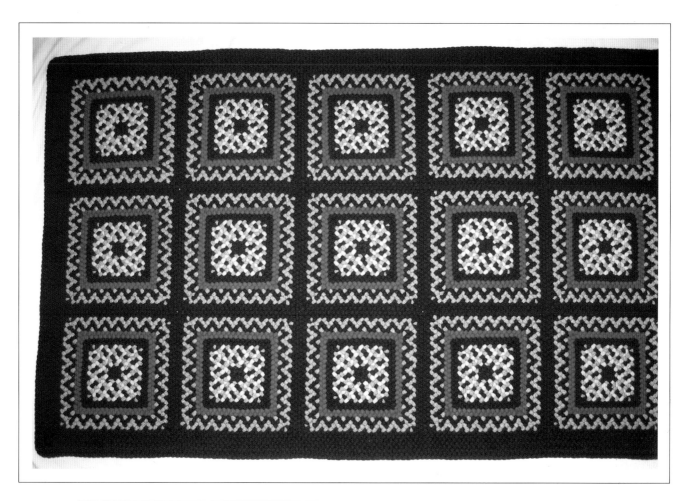

Designer: **Kay M. Gregorich**

Kay Gregorich is a relative newcomer to braiding, having learned the craft in 2003. She was already hooking rugs when she saw Rocky Mountain Rug Braider's Guild members braiding at a "hook in". She received instructions there and then went to Nancy Young's braiding camp.

Talented now in both crafts, her work encompasses a wide range of shapes and techniques. She recently entered a 28 x 70-inch (.7 x 1.8 m) runner into the Mesa County, Colorado, fair and won the Judge's Choice award and a blue ribbon.

Top:
Untitled Square, 32 x 32" (81.3 x 81.3 cm)

Bottom:
Moonflower, 73 x 45" (1.9 x 1.1 m)

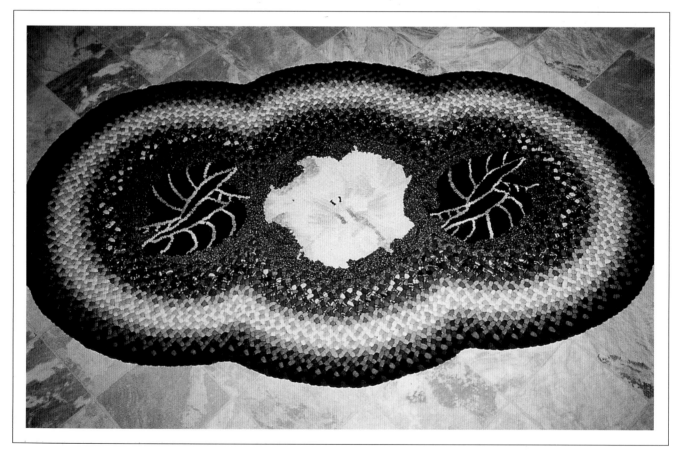

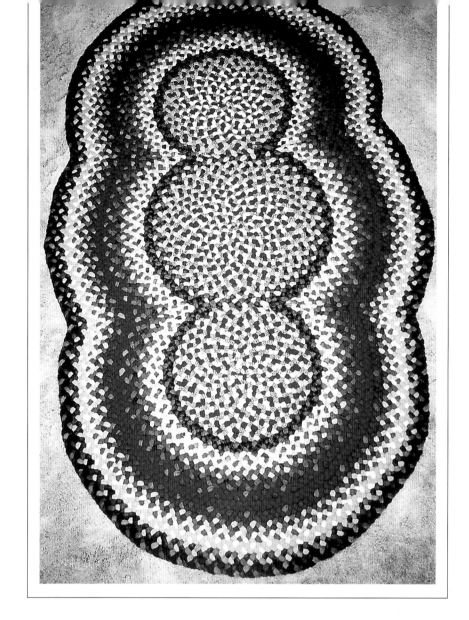

Top:
Three Circle Rug, 73 x 45" (1.9 x 1.1 m)

Right:
Ma and Pa Crow, 22 x 31 ¹/2" (55.9 x 80 cm)
Pattern by Ramona Orihill, REO Designs

Designer: **Maryann Hanson**

Maryann Hanson learned to braid from her mother, at a very young age. For nearly 70 years now, her passion has been braiding beautiful, custom-colored rugs for family and friends across the country.

She has traveled up and down the eastern seaboard, teaching braiding. She hopes to keep the fine craft and tradition of braiding alive for many generations to come.

Top: Beautiful Browns, 10 x 12'
(3.1 x 3.7 m)

Bottom: Blue, White, and Navy Blue
Oval, 3 x 5' (91.4 x 152.4 cm)

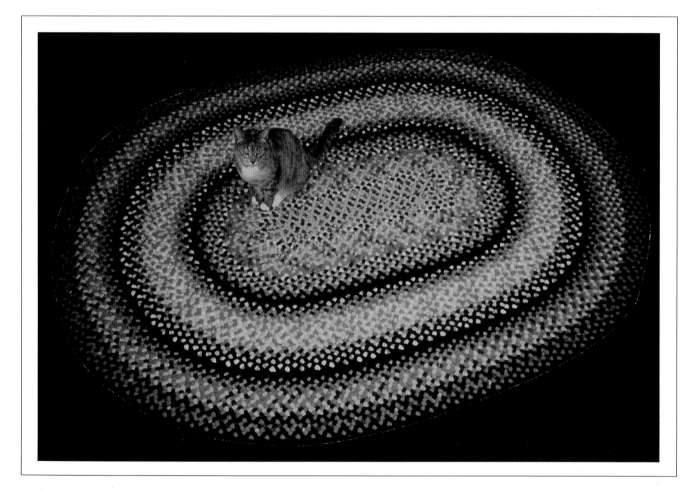

Top: Blue Circles, 3' (91.4 cm) round

Bottom left: Sunflower, 3 $^1/_2$'
(106.7 cm) round

Bottom right: Peter Rabbit, 3 $^1/_2$'
(106.7cm) round

Delsie Hoyt is the fourth generation of women in her Northeast Kingdom, Vermont, family to braid woolen rugs. She was originally inspired by the complex artistry her great-grandmother brought to this craft over a century ago. She has an original circa 1900 rug made by her and a copy of it as well, made by her great-aunt in the 1930s. Her innovative "pinwheel" design broke all rug-making conventions at the time. Delsie tries to bring that spirit and playfulness to her own braiding. She is one of today's creative and progressive braiders. Her designs attempt to explore and challenge the limitation of the braided rug form.

Delsie teaches rug braiding on a regular basis. She makes both traditional and unique braided rugs at her Kingdom Moon Rugs studio.

Top: Delsie Hoyt with a few of her creations
Photo © Jon Gilbert Fox

Bottom: Day's End, 3 x 7' (.9 x 2.1 m)
Photo © Charley Frieberg

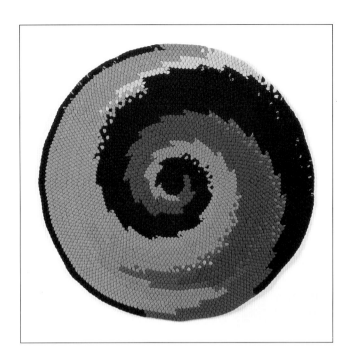

Top left: Vortex #2, 36"
(91.4 cm) round
Photo © John Gilbert Fox

Top right: Summer Morning, 40"
(101.6 cm) round
Photo © Charley Frieberg

Bottom left : The Great Wave, 40"
(101.6 cm) round
Photo © Charley Frieberg

Designer: **Janice Jurta**

Janice Jurta owns Country Braid House in Tilton, New Hampshire, a thriving business that was started as a part-time hobby by her father-in-law, George Jurta, who died in 1986. Country Braid House makes and sells high-quality braided rugs. A former administrative assistant and legal secretary, Janice began working in the shop in 1985. Her designs and marketing ideas have since helped the business increase its production from two rugs a month to three or more a week.

The rugs are made partly by the machines her father-in-law designed and patented in 1968. The cutting machine cuts and folds the woolen strips, and the winding machine winds the strips onto bobbins that fit into the braiding machine. Janice's employees hand-lace the braids together.

Most Country Braid House rugs are custom-designed, and the wool comes primarily from New Hampshire firms. Her rugs have appeared in *House and Garden* magazine. They are highly sought after by interior designers.

Top: Country Braid House, Tilton, New Hampshire

Middle: Braided Stair Runner, 30" x 20' (.76 x 6.1 m)
Photo © Martha MacEmerson

Bottom: 7-Circle Braided Runner, 29" x 10' (.74 x 3.1 m)
Photo © Charley Freiberg

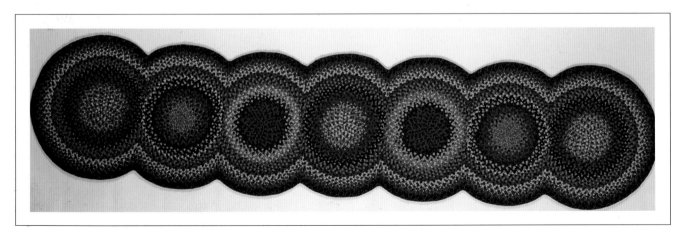

Top: Multi-Corde Rectangular Braided Rug,
10 x 14' (3.1 x 4.3 m)
Photo © Ned Scott

Bottom: Multi-Hexagon Braided Run,
7 $^1/_2$ x 11' (2.3 x 3.4 m)
Photo © Ned Scott

Designer: **Donna McKeever**

Donna McKeever says she was destined to braid because it suits her so well. With a background in computer training, Donna deals well with the challenges involved in creating functional works of art. The braiding world is indeed fortunate that she enjoys this craft.

Top: Purple and Green with Multi-Strand Border, 93 x 121" (2.4 x 3.1 m)

Bottom left: Hooked Pumpkin with Braided Border, 21" (53.3 cm) round

Bottom right: Green and Burgundy 3-Circle Rug, 43 x 78" (1.1 x 2 m)

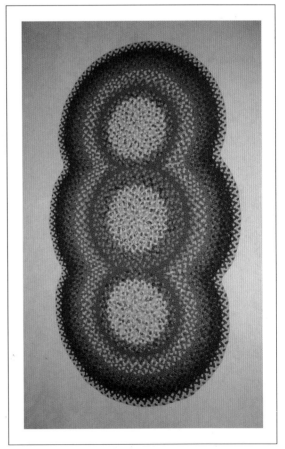

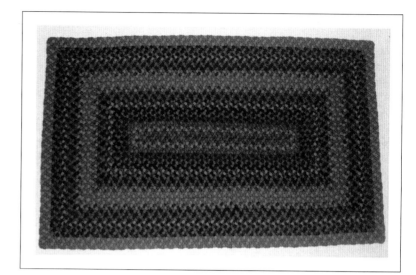

Top: Red, Green, and Gold Rectangle, 31 x 55"
(80 x 137.7 cm)

Bottom: Black, Red, Grey, Green with Multi-Strand Border,
38 x 52" (96.5 x 132.1 cm)

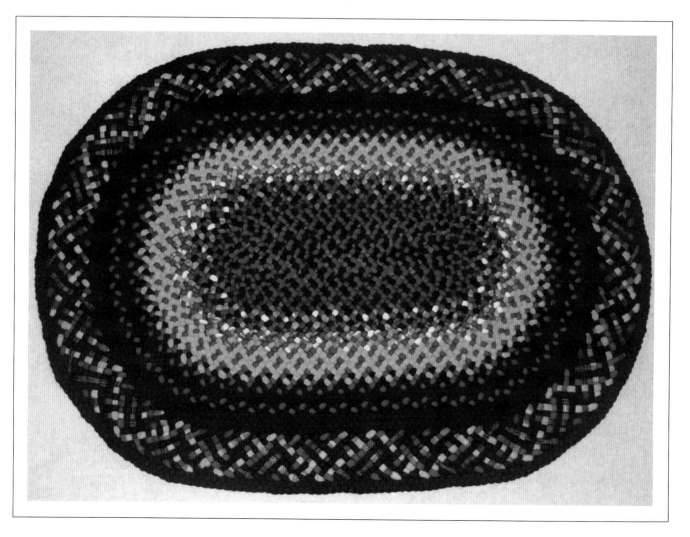

Designers: **Kate Turner** and **Cindy Barnard**
Photos © Dan Barnard

Kate and Cindy have been braiding since 1976, when they took a class together, sponsored by the New Hampshire League of Craftsmen. They now teach, in an effort to rekindle an interest in what they consider to be an important craft. And yes, they are teaching classes sponsored by the New Hampshire League of Craftsmen, where they began 30 years ago.

Top: Kate Turner (left) and Cindy Barnard (right) and their rugs

Bottom: Kate Turner, *Christmas rug,* 24 x 36" (55.9 x 91 cm)

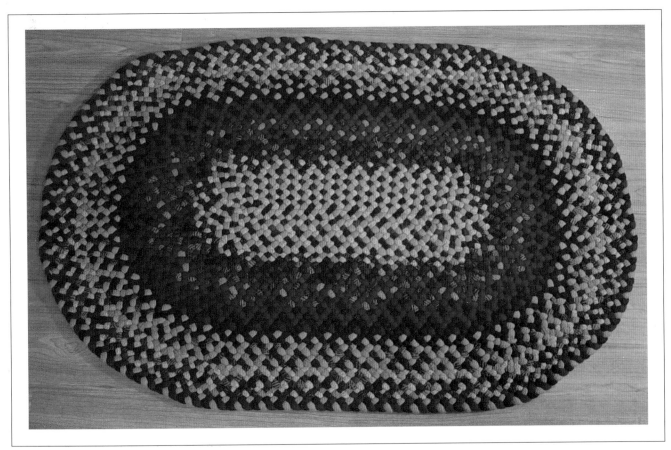

Top: Cindy Barnard, *Wedding Present*, 3 x 5' (.9 x 1.5 m)

Bottom: Cindy Barnard, *First Big Rug*, 5 x 7' (1.5 x 2.1 m)

Designer: Maxine Ward

In the late 1940s, Mrs. Iva Carroll, an elderly Ozark woman, taught Jean Will how to braid up to 21 strands. Jean then went on to teach many others how to braid in that multi-strand manner, but very few of her students continued braiding. Maxine Ward is a talented, rare exception.

Her rugs are made of coat- and blanket-weight100% wool. Maxine braids from three to 23 stands in a single rug. They are spliced/butted so that each row makes a continuous circle. She calls the wide band "the focal braid." It is composed of the colors used in the rug and makes a design like a gracefully turning ribbon.

Maxine's persistence has created a new design dimension for braiders, and she graciously shares her technique with others.

Top: Maxine Ward holding *Birthday Surprise,*
5 x 6 ^{2}/3' (1.5 x 2 m)

Bottom: Carousel, 6 ^{1}/2' (2 m) round

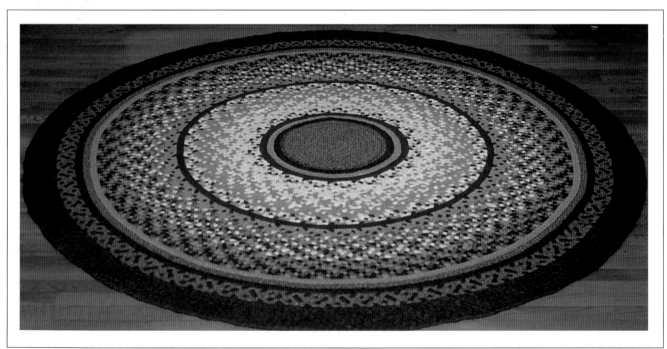

*Top: Winner's Circle, 6 $\frac{1}{2}$'
(1.98 m) round*

*Bottom: Beautiful Thing,
12 $\frac{1}{3}$ x 9' (3.8 x 2.7 m)*

Designer: **Nancy Young**
Photos © Angelique Dunn

What began as a young mother's interest in both braiding and furnishing her family's home nearly 50 years ago evolved into a lifetime of teaching, demonstrating, and also writing. For 10 years, Nancy's braided-rug newsletter linked the braiding community, as it explored every aspect of braiding. In 1994, she started the first-ever braided rug camp at her Maine lakeside home. She fashioned it after rug-hooking camps that she had attended.

Her mission now is to find museums that will officially recognize braiding as they do other fiber arts and to encourage them to display braided rugs on their walls, not just on their floors.

Top: Nancy on her deck with her *Color Wheel rug* 48" (1.2 m) round.

Bottom: Scalloped Circle, 31" (78.7 cm) round

Top: Roving Heart with 9-Strand Border,
38 x 31" (96.5 x 78.7 cm)

Bottom: Persian Square,
27" (68.6 cm)

Designer: Nancy Young

Top: Hall Runner,
5 x 9' (1.5 x 2.7 m)

Bottom: Multi-Colored Square,
35" (88.9 cm)

Lesson Plan

▼ ▼ ▼

$\mathscr{I}$ have included the following lesson plan for readers interested in teaching rug braiding. This plan has worked for me. It shows the steps needed to finish a rug in six weeks.

Lesson 1

1. Talk about wool, equipment, cost, design, and use of color.

2. Explain how to measure for the size rug you want.

3. Show samples of steps in making the *T*. Pass out practice strips; start braiding the *T*.

4. Pass out Braid-Klamps; talk about Braid-Aids, and distribute, if requested.

5. Practice braiding; teach corner turn, and how to add another strip of wool.

6. Teach how to count five rows.

7. Assignment for next week: Purchase wool, repeat *T*, braid 13 inches (33.5 cm), turn the corner, and braid as much as you can (up to five rows).

Lesson 2

1. Teach center lacing, then teach lacing technique for the rest of the rug.

2. Show how to make a square knot.

3. Teach color change.

4. Assignment for next week: Finish lacing five rows, change color, and continue braiding.

Lessons 3 and 4

1. Check on progress of lacing and other techniques.

2. Continue braiding, lacing, and changing colors.

3. Assignment for next week: Braid and lace ten rows.

4. Be ready to rattail in class at the end of row 15.

Lesson 5

1. Do rattailing.

1. Show how to start butting..

3. Assignment for next week: Start to butt; braid and lace around rug for one or two rows.

Lesson 6

1. Butt one or two rows.

2. Celebrate the students' completion of their rugs. Photograph the rugs.

Wallace Nutting, *A Fairie Tale*

Qualities of a Well-Made Braided Rug

▼ ▼ ▼

I am often asked what qualities to look for in a well-made braided rug. Here are the tips and techniques I've learned over the years that are my standards:

- Rugs should have an interesting and pleasing overall look.

- Wool is, by far, preferable to cotton, synthetics, etc.

- All wool strands must be even in weight.

- Rows should always be the same width.

- Color changes on an oval should be on the end of the same curve.

- When changing colors, make sure all seams are hidden under the preceding loop.

- Both ends of the rug should be the same size.

- The sides of an oval should be parallel.

- Never skip on the sides of an oval.

- Skips on the end of an oval, and on a circle, should be evenly distributed, with no obvious flat spots.

- Skips on a circle should be evenly distributed around the perimeter.

- Lacing thread should never show.

- Lacing every loop is preferable to lacing every other loop on the straight side of the rug.

- As you are lacing, constantly watch that your rug is lying flat, with no humps or wavy edges. Stop immediately if you do notice humps or wavy edges because this is an indication that you have skipping problems. The hump means you have not skipped enough. Unfortunately, you will need to take out your lacing back to the beginning of the hump, and then re-lace. Wavy edges mean you have skipped too much. This can be fixed by lacing without skipping on your next row.

- Not many "tweaks." An area on an individual braid that is not rounded and shows a crease or a dent is a tweak. Tweaks are usually the result of using wool that is too light in weight.

- Occasionally check both sides of your rug to make sure folds are not showing. You are always looking at the top of the rug, so it is important to remind yourself to make sure the back side of the rug is looking beautiful too.

- If you want drastic color changes, you will need to butt your rug. Remember, once you start butting, you can't go back to a continuous braid.

- Rattail and butting should be fairly invisible.

And, the ultimate test of your braiding technique is:

- When you drop your rug on the floor, it should land flat.

Glossary

Banana-shaped
A rug that isn't straight; both ends curve in one direction.

Band
Several rows of braid using the same color combinations.

Barbells
An oval rug with ends that bulge, the result of skipping on the straight sides before the curve should begin or after the curve should end.

Braid
Three tubes braided together.

Buckling
Not enough skips. This is quite common for beginners. It forces the center of the rug up and the edges up (into a hat shape). The only remedy is to take out the lacing until the rug is flat. Make sure you skip more often when relacing.

Butting
Method of joining the beginning of a row to the end so that it forms a complete circle. This gives the rug a finished look. Usually used for the last two rows. Can be used for all or part of a rug.

Continuous braid
The way almost all rugs are made. Keep braiding, forming a spiral. You braid, lace, change colors, add new strips, and braid again to make the rug larger and larger.

Fold
The side of the tube that has the raw edges turned in towards the center.

Hit-or-miss rug
Braided with small strands of wool of various colors randomly scattered throughout the rug.

Lacing
Method of attaching the new braid to the body of the rug.

Lacing needles
Needles designed for lacing braided rugs. There is a variety available. Braid-Aid has a lacer that is easy to use because it has a flat, curved design. Rounded, tipped tapestry needles are also good.

Lacing thread
Such as three-ply Irish linen for lacing small items. This would be good for a mat or a chair pad. A rug calls for a heavier lacing thread, such as six-ply Irish linen.

Loop
One of the three tubes after it has been braided.

Multi-strand braid
Using more than three strands or tubes braided together.

Plaiting
The dominant braiding method used many years ago, and still being used today. It is a flat, folded braid. It produces a fold on the back side, and the side of the braid is straight.

Pulled loop
After braiding twice overs, the single loop on the opposite side is pulled tightly, therefore called a pulled loop.

Rattailing or tapering
Method of ending a continuous braided rug.

Reverse *e*
One method of lacing the first row; named because the thread forms an *e* in reverse.

Row
Three loops braided and laced to a rug.

Scallops
Too many skips make the rug raise up and down. To resolve, don't skip at all on the next row. This will usually flatten it out.

Shoulder
The beginning and end of the curve.

Skip
When lacing on the curved end of the rug (or all around a circle rug), you have to routinely skip one loop on the row you are attaching in order to make a flat, well-shaped rug.

Strand or strip
One length of wool ready to braid.

T-start
The method used to begin the rug.

Tweaks
Dents/folds in your tube. Tweaks usually occur when braiding with lightweight wool.

Tube
A strip of wool after the edges have been turned in.

Twice overs
Braiding twice from one side then once from the other side.

V
Formed by braiding twice overs in both the top and bottom of heart-shaped rug.

Weight
The number of pounds of wool per yard. Medium-weight wool is 16 ounces per pound. I recommend that you try to use approximately the same weight wool throughout the rug.

Working braid
The braid you are attaching to the rug.

Bibliography

▼ ▼ ▼

Baker, M.E. *Purveyor of Nostalgia—Wallace Nutting's Southbury Connections.* Connecticut: The Newtown Bee, 1984.

Carter, Mary Randolph. *American Family Style.* New York: Viking Studio Books, 1988.

Carty, Sally Clarke. *How to Make Braided Rugs.* New York: McGraw-Hill Book Company, 1977.

Cox, Verna P. *Braided Rug Manual.* Bucksport, Maine: Self-published, 1967.

Feeley, Helen Howard. *The Complete Book of Rug Braiding.* New York: Coward-McCann, Inc., 1957.

Gordon, Beverly. *Shaker Textile Arts.* Hanover, New Hampshire: University Press of New England, 1980.

Horsham, Michael. *The Art of the Shakers.* New Jersey: Chartwell Books, 1989.

Ivankovich, Michael. *The Guide to Wallace Nutting Furniture.* Doylestown, Pennsylvania: Diamond Press, 1990.

Kopp, Joel and Kate. *American Hooked and Sewn Rugs, Folk Art Underfoot.* New York: E.P. Dutton, Inc., 1985.

Lipman, Jean and Winchester, Alice. *The Flowering of American Folk Art (1776-1876).* Pennsylvania: Courage Books, 1974.

Little, Nina Fletcher. *Floor Coverings in New England Before 1850.* Massachusetts: Old Sturbridge Village, 1967.

Manroe, Candace Ord. *Shaker Style, The Gift of Simplicity.* New York: Crescent Books, 1991.

Nutting, Wallace. *Connecticut Beautiful.* Framingham, Massachusetts: Old America Company, 1923.

Rebus, Inc. *American Country, The Needle Arts.* Alexandria, Virginia: Time-Life Books, 1990.

Stockhaus, Peter. *Little Book of Early American Crafts and Trades.* New York: Dover Publications, Inc., 1976.

Tudor, Tasha. *The Dolls' Christmas.* New York: Henry Z. Walck, Inc., 1950.

Weissman, Judith Reiter and Lavitt, Wendy. *Labors of Love, America's Textiles and Needlework, 1650-1930.* New York: Alfred A. Knopf, 1987.

A NOTE ABOUT SUPPLIERS

Usually, the supplies you need for making the projects in Lark books can be found at your local craft supply store, discount mart, home improvement center, or retail shop relevant to the topic of the book. Occasionally, however, you may need to buy materials or tools from specialty suppliers. In order to provide you with the most up-to-date information, we have created a list of suppliers on our website, which we update on a regular basis. Visit us at www.larkbooks.com, click on "Craft Supply Sources," and then click on the relevant topic. You will find numerous companies listed with their web address and/or mailing address and phone number.

Index

▼ ▼ ▼

Index of Artists

▼ ▼ ▼